KEN AKAMATSU

vol.27

CHARACTERS

KURŌMARU TOKISAKA

UQ HOLDER NO. 11

A skilled fencer of the Shinmei school. A member of the Yata no Karasu tribe of immortal hunters who will be neither male nor female until a coming of age ceremony at age sixteen.

KIRIË SAKURAME

UQ HOLDER NO. 9

The greatest financial contributor to UQ Holder. She has the unique skill Reset & Restart, which allows her to go back to a save point when she dies. She can stop time by kissing Tōta.

KARIN YŪKI

UQ HOLDER NO. 4

Can withstand any attack without receiving a single scratch. Her immortality is S-class. Also known as the Saintess of Steel.

TŌTA KONOE

UQ HOLDER NO. 7

An immortal vampire. Has the ability Magia Erebea as well the only power that can defeat the Mage of Beginning, the White of Mars (Magic Cancel) hidden inside him.

UQ HOLDER IMMORTAL NUMBERS

JINBEI SHISHIDO

UQ HOLDER NO. 2

UQ Holder's oldest member. Has the "Switcheroo" skill that switches the locations of physical objects.

SEPT SHICHIJŪRŌ NANAO

UQ HOLDER NO. E

UQ Holder's talented butler, and Ba'al's most prized creation. A high-level artificial light spirit.

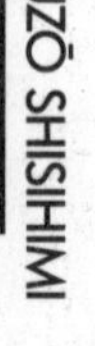

JŪZŌ SHISHIMI

UQ HOLDER NO. 5

The Numbers' most skilled swordsman. Can slice through even intangible concepts.

Ken Akamatsu Presents

IALDA BAOTH

The Mage of the Beginning and the Lifemaker. Is attempting to destroy the world by casting the final spell, Cosmo Entelekheia.

EVANGELINE (YUKIHIME)

The female leader of UQ Holder and a 700-year-old vampire. Her past self met Tōta in a rift in time-space, and that encounter gave hope to her bleak immortal existence.

BA'AL

A High Daylight Walker. Once Eva's archnemesis. Number destroyed his heart, and his ethereal body with it, but 45 years ago, he suddenly attacked them again.

FATE AVERRUNCUS

Negi's sworn friend. Was once UQ Holder's enemy but now fights alongside them.

SANTA SASAKI

UQ HOLDER NO. 12

A revenant brought back to life through necromancy. He has multiple abilities.

IKKŪ AMEYA

UQ HOLDER NO. 10

An 85-year-old full-body cyborg. Has currently fallen into Ba'al's clutches.

NIKITIS LAPIS

UQ HOLDER NO. 8

A book-loving High Daylight Walker. Had once teamed up with Ba'al.

GENGORŌ MAKABE

UQ HOLDER NO. 6

He has a skill known as "multiple lives," so when he dies, another Gengorō appears.

THE STORY SO FAR

Tōta is reunited with his friends.
DON'T WORRY.
I'M SURE I'LL BE BACK IN TIME FOR DINNER.

In a fleeting moment of respite,
he gives Kurōmaru a reward. ♡
K...
KURŌ-MARU...?
A-ARE YOU OKAY?

And he gives Karin...
proof that he loves her.♡♡

I GUESS IT DOESN'T MATTER...
BE-CAUSE...
I FEEL REALLY SAFE WITH YOU NOW...
YEAH...
For Kirië, he grants a sense of security. ♡♡♡

CONTENTS

KARIN-CHAN!
KIRIË!
I'M SO GLAD... TO SEE YOU'RE OKAY.
I'M GLAD YOU'RE OKAY, TOO, KARIN-CHAN.
I DIDN'T THINK I'D EVER GET TO SEE YOU AGAIN.
KURŌ-MARU...
KIRIË-CHAN, IT'S SO GOOD TO SEE YOU...
<FEMALE

STAGE 185: COMMENCING OPERATION
BEFORE WE REUNITE YOU WITH ALL THE OTHERS,
I WOULD LIKE TO HOLD A BRIEFING SESSION OF THE UQ GIRLS MUTUAL ALLIANCE.
WHAT?
UH...
WAIT A...
HOLD IT RIGHT THERE, NANAKO. WHAT IS THIS ABOUT?
A VERY IMPORTANT MATTER.
THE QUES-TION IS...
HOW FAR HAS EACH OF YOU GONE WITH TŌTA-SAMA?
WE'LL START WITH YOU, KARIN-SAMA.
HUH ?!
JUST A-
WINCE...
B-DMP
WHAT THE HECK ARE YOU ASKING OUT OF THE BLUE?!

F-FIRST OF ALL, I HAVEN'T DONE *ANYTHING* WITH HIM, SO...
HUH ...?

WHAT?
TO BE SPECIFIC, I HAVEN'T DONE ANYTHING WITH HIM SINCE WE GOT BACK FROM ALPHA CENTAURI, I SWEAR.

HUH...? THEN THAT MEANS YOU...
MWOM
ほわん
MWOM
ほわ～ん

IN SPACE ...?
GULP
IN ZERO GRAVITY?
ZE... ZERO GRAVITY ...!!
WE DIDN'T DO ANYTHING FREAKY THAT REQUIRED ZERO GRAVITY, OKAY!

LIAR! YOU DID! YOU TOTALLY DID!
W-W-W-W-WE DID NOT!

THEN LET'S PHRASE THE QUESTION MORE PRECISELY.
KARIN-CHAN. HOW MANY TIMES DID YOU DO IT?
DON'T SAY IT LIKE THAT!

SO...? HOW WAS IT?
H-HOW AM I SUPPOSED TO ANSWER THAT...?

MM-HM.

HNGH...
カァ
BLUSH

...
...TIMES.
WHAT?
EIGH... ● TIMES.
FIDGET
WELL, WELL...
PSST
WALLA
IN FIVE HOURS...
KARIN-CHAN IS SURPRISINGLY...
THAT'S... WOW.
WOULD YOU PLEASE NOT WHISPER TO EACH OTHER LIKE THAT?
WHAT ABOUT *YOU*, KIRIË?
WHAT?!
WE WERE KEEPING TABS ON YOU, YOU KNOW.
URK!
WE ALREADY KNOW THE TWO OF YOU HARDLY LEFT YOUR PENTHOUSE AT ALL FOR FIVE DAYS AFTER HE FOUND YOU.
WHAT WERE YOU DOING, I WONDER?

I HAD TO TALK, SO NOW IT'S YOUR TURN.
RUMBLE
RUMBLE
RUMBLE
I NEED A PLACE AND A NUMBER.
YOU'RE SCARING ME!
YOU'RE SCARING ME, KARIN-CHAN!

MM-HMMM. WAIT...THE KITCHEN?
BUT WHAT KIND OF...?
I MEAN, YOU KNOW...
YOU JUST GO WITH THE FLOW AND THINGS... HAPPEN, RIGHT?

QUITE RISQUE.
HOW EROTIC.
VERY NAUGHTY.
I CAN HEAR YOU, YOU KNOW!

AND?
URGH.

UM... WELL.
I MEAN...
TW...
TIMES.

AND HERE I WAS HOLDING BACK OUT OF CONSIDERATION FOR YOU, AND THE FACT THAT WE DIDN'T KNOW WHERE YOU WERE. YOU'VE GOT SOME NERVE...
I'M SORRY! I'M REALLY SORRY, KARIN-CHAN!
SNEEEAK

KURŌ-MARU?
YOU CAN TRY TO RUN, BUT YOU WON'T GET AWAY.
RUMBLE
RUMBLE
EEEK!
YIPE
TALK.
MM-HMM... WAIT. A HOT SPRING, UNDER THE STARS WITH FLOWER PETALS DANCING IN THE AIR?
IN THE WATER...?
UM ...

NO FAIR, KURŌ-MARU! HOW COME YOU HAD A ROMANTIC EXPERI-ENCE?!
NOT BAD, KURŌMARU! I'M REALLY IMPRESSED!
UM... WAS THIS SOME KIND OF COMPETI-TION...?
STUUUNN
DU-DUN

AND...?
UM!
ER!
ZOOM

D-DO I HAVE TO TELL ...?
DAMN RIGHT YOU DO!
UM, I... I DON'T REMEM-BER EXACT-LY...
THEN YOUR BEST GUESS!
WELL... UM.
I...
SHUDDER

I THINK ...
...IT WAS
... TIMES.
WHAT?
SI...
SE...
● TIMES.
MAYBE.
...
カアア…
BLUUUSH

WHAT KIND OF A NUMBER IS THAT ?!
ズバ
KA-BAM
THAT'S TOO HOT! THAT'S TOO MUCH, KURŌMARU!
HOW THIRSTY ARE YOU?!
KURŌMARU-SAMA WINS!!
パパ
PA-POP!
NO! I THINK IT'S JUST, WITH THE WAY I AM PHYSICALLY, IT'S EASIER FOR CERTAIN THINGS TO HAPPEN, SO SPEAKING IN TERMS OF TIME, I DON'T THINK IT WAS THAT DIFFERENT FROM EITHER OF...
THAT'S EVEN DIRTIER!!

HUFF ...
HUFF ...

WAS THERE A POINT IN THIS "BRIEFING SESSION"?
SUD-DENLY I'M SUPER TIRED.
DU-DUN
OF COURSE.
...
BUT ARE YOU OKAY WITH THIS, KIRIË?
HUH?

THE DEAL WE MADE IS NOT NORMAL FROM AN ORDINARY HUMAN'S PERSPEC-TIVE.
WE ONLY MADE IT BECAUSE, AS IMMORTALS, WE WON'T BE TYING HIM DOWN WITH FINITE TIME.
YOU'RE AN ORDINARY HUMAN NOW.
...

OH, IS THAT WHAT YOU'RE WORRIED ABOUT?
OF COURSE I'M OKAY WITH IT.
I WANT TO BE FRIENDS WITH BOTH OF YOU FOR AS LONG AS I CAN, TOO.

HUG
ギュッ
HUG
きゅっ
IF HE STAYS WITH ME UNTIL I DIE LIKE HE SAYS HE WILL...
...I'LL BE WITH YOU TWO UNTIL THEN, TOO.

OK, KIRIË-CHAN.
SO...
...DON'T EITHER OF YOU DISAPPEAR ON ME, OKAY?
WE WON'T.

HUUUGG

WOW, THIS SHIP IS HUGE.
SO WHERE IS EVERY-BODY?

AFTER TŌTA GOT BACK AND STARTED LOOKING AROUND, A DOOR THAT WOULDN'T OPEN DECIDED TO OPEN.
THEY'RE ALL IN THERE LOOKING FOR CLUES.
BASICALLY, THIS IS WHERE NEGI SPRING-FIELD...

...WHERE TŌTA'S GRANDFATHER WAS DOING HIS FINAL RESEARCH. HIS MAIN WORKSHOP.
KIRIË-CHAN!
SANTA!

I'M SO GLAD YOU'RE ALIVE...
HUUUGG
ぎゅっ
NOT TECHNICALLY ALIVE, BUT YEAH.
YOU GOT TALLER, KIRIË-CHAN.

IT'S GOOD TO SEE YOU, KIRIË.
CONGRATULATIONS ON MAKING IT BACK.

WOW, I DIDN'T EXPECT TO EVER SEE *THAT* LOOK ON YOUR FACE.
I GUESS YOU'VE MELLOWED OUT SOME, GENGORŌ?
SAME TO YOU, KIRIË.
TŌTA TOLD ME WHAT HAPPENED.

SO...WOULD YOU MIND TELLING ME A LITTLE ABOUT THAT WORLD YOU WERE IN SOMETIME?

HUH? SURE, I DON'T MIND. BUT I DON'T THINK THERE'S ANYTHING ABOUT IT THAT WOULD INTEREST YOU.

HMMM-MMM-MMM-MM-MMMM.
WELL?

DID YOU FIND ANYTHING?
THERE ARE THOUSANDS OF NOTE-BOOKS HERE. IT'S REALLY HARD JUST READING THEM ALL.
BUT YOU DON'T HAVE TO GET FAR BEFORE A TON OF INTERESTING STUFF POPS UP.
THAT'S MY GRANDPA FOR YOU.
STILL...IF YOU'RE ASKING ABOUT A DECISIVE CLUE TO HELP US FIGURE OUT HOW TO BEAT IALDA...

YOU HAVEN'T FOUND ONE, HAVE YOU?
THERE HAS TO BE SOME-THING...
SOMETHING GRANDPA WANTED TO LEAVE BEHIND, SOME KIND OF MESSAGE...

WELL, WE'RE GOING TO HAVE TO FIGHT WHETHER WE FIND ONE OR NOT...

...
YEAH.
YOU'RE RIGHT.

...IF WE'RE GOING TO SAVE THE WORLD.

WELL, WELL!
WHAT HAVE WE HERE?

LOOK.
I FOUND THIS IN THIS HOLLOW BOOK.

WHAT IS IT?
IT'S...
A POCKET-BOOK?
HMMM.

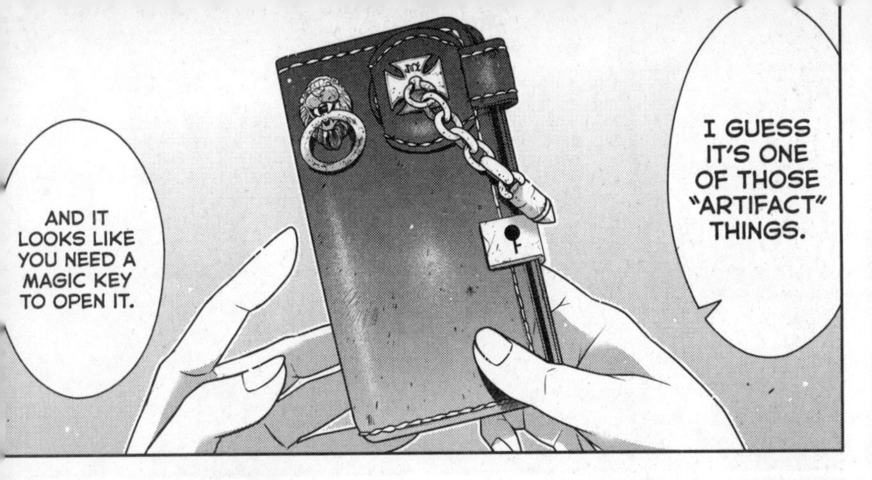
I GUESS IT'S ONE OF THOSE "ARTIFACT" THINGS.
AND IT LOOKS LIKE YOU NEED A MAGIC KEY TO OPEN IT.

HOLD ON. THERE'S AN ADDRESS HERE IN THE HOLLOW BOOK.
HUH?
THIS IS NEAR OUR OLD HIDEOUT.
LET'S SEE HERE.

RRT

ERRRT
ERRRT
WHAT THE?
AN ALARM?
ERRRT

ALL NUMBERS, REPORT TO THE BRIDGE!
THIS IS AN EMERGENCY!
ERRRT
ERRRT

I REPEAT. ALL NUMBERS, REPORT TO THE BRIDGE! THIS IS AN EMERGENCY!
AN EMERGENCY...
ERRRT

YOU'RE TOO SLOW.
GET HERE IN TWO SECONDS.
THAT'S NOT EVEN POSSIBLE.
NANAKO CAN DO IT.

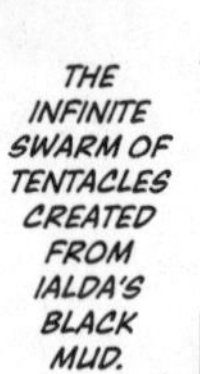

WE'RE GETTING A TRANS-MISSION FROM FATE.
SNAP
PEOPLE OF UQ HOLDER. I'M HERE TO TELL YOU THAT THERE HAS BEEN MOVEMENT ON PLUTO.
VNN
EIGHT HOURS AGO,
WE LOST CONTACT WITH 17 OF OUR SURVEILLANCE SHIPS IN PLUTO'S ORBIT.
FLASH
WE DON'T KNOW EXACTLY WHAT IS GOING ON IN THAT AREA.
THESE ARE OPTICAL IMAGES TAKEN FROM SATURN.
FLASH
WE HAVE BEEN INVESTIGATING PLUTO FOR 40 YEARS AND YET FAILED TO FIND EVEN A TRACE OF THEM.
BUT NOW THESE HAVE REAP-PEARED.
THE INFINITE SWARM OF TENTACLES CREATED FROM IALDA'S BLACK MUD.
FURTHERMORE, AN ENORMOUS AMOUNT OF MAGICAL ENERGY IS COLLECTING AROUND PLUTO AT A SPEED THAT IS THEORETICALLY IMPOSSIBLE.
EVERYTHING IS HAPPENING MUCH FASTER THAN IT EVER HAS BEFORE. WE WILL NOT BE ABLE TO DEPLOY OUR FLEET IN TIME.
S-SO YOU'RE SAYING THAT COSMO ENTELE-KHEIA IS...

EXACTLY.
WE BELIEVE THAT IALDA BAOTH, THE MAGE OF THE BEGINNING,
HAS ENTERED THE FINAL STAGES IN THE ACTIVATION OF COSMO ENTELEKHEIA.
WE DON'T KNOW WHEN IT WILL BEGIN, BUT WHEN IT DOES, THAT WILL BE THE END.

UNLESS WE DO SOMETHING, THEN WE ONLY HAVE A FEW DAYS...
...BEFORE THE END OF THE WORLD.

SO IN OTHER WORDS...
YUKIHIME HAS ALREADY...
GRR
WELL, FATE?
YOU HAVE A PLAN?
YES.

WE WOULD LIKE YOU IMMORTALS TO FORM AN ADVANCE PARTY TO JUMP TO PLUTO AND BEGIN THE ASSAULT.
ATTACK
Pluto
BEGIN ATTACK UPON ARRIVAL IN FIVE HOURS.
WILL ARRIVE IN ABOUT A WEEK.
UQ HOLDER NUMBERS
SOLAR SYSTEM'S MAIN FLEET
Saturn
Uranus
Neptune
Jupiter
Earth
Sun
Mars
IDEALLY YOU CAN HOLD HER OFF UNTIL THE SOLAR SYSTEM'S MAIN FLEET ARRIVES.
WE'LL USE THE JACOB'S LADDER SYSTEM TO GET YOU THERE.

...
BY ALL RIGHTS, IT SHOULD BE HUMANS WORKING TO SOLVE THIS PROBLEM.
YOU MAY FEEL NO OBLIGATION TO SAVE THE WORLD, BUT...
FATE, YOU SON OF A...
WHOOSH
ALL RIGHT.
WE'LL DO IT.
YOU DON'T MIND IF WE BEAT THEM BEFORE YOUR FLEET GETS THERE, RIGHT?
GNN

TŌTA, YOU SON OF A...!
YOU WITH ME, GUYS?

ZSH

ZAM

WAKE UP HONOKA KONOE AND ISANA KONOE.
GRIN
GO TO THE RARE BOOK COLLECTION IN THE CENTRAL CORE BLOCK, AND ONTO THE GREAT PARU SAMA DOCKED IN ITS HANGAR.
HMPH. FINE.
HUH?

PSHHH
HONO-
KA!
ISANA!
FSHHH
YOU...
I CAN'T
BELIEVE
YOU'RE
STILL
HERE...
THEY DID
OCCASIONALLY
WAKE UP FROM
COLD SLEEP
TO FIGHT
FOR US,
SO I
THINK THEY
MAY HAVE
MATURED
SOME FROM
WHAT YOU
REMEMBER,
TŌTA-SAMA.

THEY'VE BEEN WAITING FOR YOUR REVIVAL, READY FOR THE FINAL SHOWDOWN THAT IS TO COME.
OH... OKAY.

NNN ...
UH...

NII-SAMA!
WHAM
YO!
KURŌ-MARU-SEMPAI!
SQUEEZE
H-HELLO.

...BUT
HONO-KA, ISANA.
IS THIS REALLY WHAT YOU WANT?
TO SKIP SO MANY YEARS, WHEN YOU'RE NOT IMMORTAL ...?
WHAT ABOUT YOUR FRIENDS AND FAMILY?

OUR GRAND-MOTHERS ARE UP THERE.
FREEING OUR GRANDFATHER, OUR GRAND-MOTHERS, AND ALL THEIR FRIENDS...
THAT'S OUR DREAM AND OUR MISSION.

SO... THIS IS IT.
TIME FOR THE FINAL SHOW-DOWN.
OH RIGHT. THIS WILL BE YOUR FIRST TIME FIGHTING IALDA, WON'T IT?
YEAH.

JACOB'S LADDER PROJECT CENTRAL FACILITY, DISTORTION FIELD GENERATOR RINGS
オ。

DON'T WORRY.
WE'RE JUST GOING TO DO WHAT WE WOULD HAVE DONE 45 YEARS AGO IF YOU HAD BEEN WITH US.
YEAH...
THAT'S RIGHT.

WE'RE GOING TO SAVE THE WORLD, SAVE HUMAN-KIND...
AND RESCUE GRAND-PA...
AND YUKI-HIME.
YEAH.
TŌTA.

YOU WON'T BE ABLE TO CALL US ONCE THE MISSION HAS STARTED.
SPEAK.
TŌTA!

KIRIË! WHERE ARE YOU?

WELL, WE MADE IT TO THE CAPITAL.
IT REALLY BRINGS BACK MEMORIES.
I ASSURE YOU KIRIË-SAMA WILL BE SAFE.
SANTA-SAMA AND I WILL ACT AS HER BODYGUARDS. NOTHING OUT OF THE ORDINARY WILL BEFALL HER.
HAPPY CONES
Sweet Dlicious IceCream

NII-CHAN!
WE'LL FIND NEGI-SAN'S SECRET WEAPON, THEN I'LL BE RIGHT BEHIND YOU, I PROMISE.
I KNOW.
I'M COUNTING ON YOU, SANTA.
ALL RIGHT, THEN. YOU DO YOUR JOB UP THERE.

I'LL BE WAITING FOR YOU, TŌTA.

YEAH.

I PROMISE I'LL BE BACK.
KIRIË.
MISSION STARTING IN 80.
OKAY, LITTLE LADIES.
TRY NOT TO MOVE TOO MUCH.

IF YOU PEEK OUTSIDE MY SERIAL SWITCHEROO SPACE, YOUR FACES'LL BE SHREDDED LIKE TEA LEAVES AND FLOAT AWAY AS SPACE DEBRIS.
Y-YES, SIR.
THAT'S A VERY GRAPHIC DESCRIP-TION, JINBEI-SAN.

YOU, TOO, GENGORO-SAN. STAY INSIDE MY REVOLUTION MAGIC.
OKAY.
BUT IN MY CASE, I'D JUST LOSE SOME LIVES.

OH? HOW MANY LIVES DO YOU HAVE NOW?
WELL, I'VE BEEN DOING A LOT OF GOOD DEEDS OVER THE LAST 45 YEARS, SO...

I'VE MAXED OUT AT 65,535 LIVES.
URK!
HOW MANY TIMES COULD YOU FINISH MARIO WITH THAT?
HEH...
HM?
SAVING THE WORLD, EH?

HOW MUCH DO YOU REALLY MEAN THAT?
TŌTA KONOE.

GUH...

WELL... I DON'T KNOW.
JACOBS LADDER PROJECT
BEFORE... I WANTED TO SAVE THE WORLD TO HELP YUKIHIME... BUT I WAS KIND OF MIXED UP ABOUT IT.
BUT... NOW...

WELL...
I REALLY JUST DON'T KNOW.
REALLY.
AS FOR ME...
I DON'T CARE ONE WAY OR ANOTHER ABOUT THE WORLD.
YEAH.
I CAN TELL.
KIRIË'S THE SAME WAY.
I DON'T HAVE A PROBLEM WITH THAT.
NO.
THAT'S NOT WHAT I MEAN.

I MEAN...
I'M NOT FROM THIS WORLD.

...
HUH?

WHAT DO YOU MEAN?
OH...DOES THIS HAVE SOMETHING TO DO WITH WHAT YOU WERE ASKING KIRIË...?
...
LAUNCHING IN 1800.
JACOBS LADDER
WE HAVE SOME TIME.
MIND LISTENING TO ME RAMBLE FOR A WHILE?
SURE, SEMPAI.
WOW, THIS IS SO UNLIKE YOU.
OKAY. WELL...

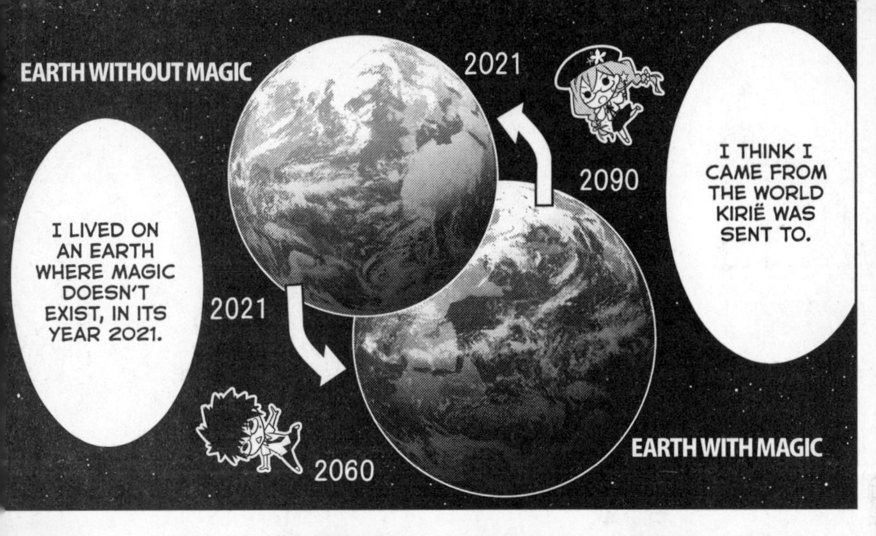
EARTH WITHOUT MAGIC
2021
2090
I THINK I CAME FROM THE WORLD KIRIË WAS SENT TO.
I LIVED ON AN EARTH WHERE MAGIC DOESN'T EXIST, IN ITS YEAR 2021.
2021
2060
EARTH WITH MAGIC

I GOT HIT BY A TRUCK IN THE OTHER WORLD.
WHAT.
KARAOKE
PARADISE
PLAY THE NEWEST GAMES
BATH
SHIN KAN-MAN
TAMI
THE NEXT THING I KNEW, I WAS IN THE MIDDLE OF A SHOOT-OUT BETWEEN THE YAKUZA AND THE MAFIA, WITH MAGIC AND BULLETS FLYING EVERYWHERE.
WHOA...

THERE WAS A POPULAR VIDEO GAME SERIES IN MY WORLD THAT WAS JUST LIKE IT.
GANGSTER GAMES WHERE YOU FIGHT WITH MAGIC, GUNS, AND FISTS.
UH-HUH.
MAFIA
7
SO, I THOUGHT
I MUST HAVE DIED AND BEEN REBORN IN THE VIDEO GAME.
WHAT THEY CALL ISEKAI REINCARNATION.
UH... GEN-GORO-SEMPAI, WHAT ARE YOU TALKING ABOUT?
OH... WERE ISEKAI STORIES NOT POPULAR IN THIS WORLD?

I SEE EVERYTHING IN THIS WORLD AS A VIDEO GAME.
I SEE YOUR STRENGTHS AND ABILITIES AS STATISTICS, TOO, TŌTA.
I CAN SEE DATA ON EVERYTHING.
TŌTA KONOE
VAMPIRE
MP(魔 75270
9999999999
LIMIT BREAK
STATUS
SPEED: 775
AVERAGE CHI: 776
CHI COEFFICIENT: ×97
AVERAGE MAGIC: 579
MAGIC COEFFICIENT: ×130
EARTH: 780
WATER: 234
FIRE: 530
WIND: 733
DARK: 998
LIGHT: 132
SKILLS:
RAPID REGENERATION SS+
DARK MAGIC A++
LOAD MAGIC A
THUNDER IN HEAVEN, GREAT VIGOR A+
LIGHTNING SPEED B+
HELL'S REFINING FIRE B
ICE FLOWER VESTIGE B
DEMON ADVENT ARMAMENT S++
BLOOD MANIPULATION S
APPRENTICE
TIME LOOPER
JACOBS LADDER PROJECT

I USED THIS POWER AND MY MULTIPLE LIVES TO CLIMB THE RANKS OF THE UNDERWORLD.
WH...

WHOA WHOA WHOA. HOLD ON. SO WHAT ARE YOU SAYING?
WE'RE ALL JUST CHARACTERS IN SOME VIDEO GAME YOU'RE PLAYING?
NO, YOU'RE NOT.
I LEARNED THAT FOR MYSELF.
YOU ALL REALLY EXIST.
AND THIS WORLD EXISTS, TOO.
THIS IS REALITY.
JACOBS LADDER PROJECT

WHAT'S MESSED UP IS MY HEAD.
YOU TALK LIKE KARIN-SEMPAI.
JACOBS LADDER PROJECT

HAVE YOU TOLD JINBEI-SAN ABOUT THIS, TOO?
NO, HE DOESN'T PLAY VIDEO GAMES.
JACOBS LADDER PROJECT

HMM-MMM...
WELL...
JACOBS LADDER

I ALWAYS WONDER.
WHAT WILL HAPPEN TO ME WHEN I RUN OUT OF LIVES?
WILL I JUST DISAPPEAR, OR WILL I GO BACK TO MY WORLD IN 2021?

...

THAT SOUNDS REALLY COOL!!

YOU THINK SO?

I ENVY ALL OF YOU.
IT'S NOT EASY TO LIVE LIKE YOU DO IN THE REALITY WHERE I COME FROM.
JACOBS LADDER PROJECT

...
SEMPAI ...

I TOLD YOU I'M READY TO DIE ANY-TIME, REMEM-BER?
THIS IS MY PATHETIC REASON FOR THAT READI-NESS.
THIS WAS NEVER MY WORLD TO BEGIN WITH.

BUT...
IN MY LIFE HERE, I FOUND PEOPLE I LIKE BEING AROUND, PEOPLE I CARE FOR.
EVEN SOMEONE I LOVED.

...
WELL.
WHAT I'M SAYING IS...

AND A TON OF EXTRA LIVES, TOO.
I HAVE THIS LIFE THAT DOESN'T MEAN MUCH,
THE PERSON I LOVED LOVED THIS WORLD.
SO I DON'T MIND USING MY LIVES TO SAVE IT.

I JUST WANTED YOU TO KNOW TH–
MRSH

KER-SKRNCH
HUB-WAGH ?!
DANGIT, SEMPAI.
TSHHHH
WHY WOULD YOU SAY ALL THESE THINGS THAT FORESHADOW YOUR OWN DEATH?
GENGORO-SEMPAI.
BLOOD MANIPULATION? NO... DID HE HIT ME WITH MIASMA?
ANOTHER STRANGE ABILITY...
JACOBS LADDER PROJECT
WHA ...?
I FELT HIS FIST THROUGH THE GLASS...?

WE'RE ALL GOING TO MAKE IT BACK TOGETHER.
YOU STILL HAVE TO HEAR THE REST JINBEI-SAN'S WAR STORIES, REMEMBER?

...
YOU'RE RIGHT, TŌTA.

ALL GREEN.
LAUNCHING IN 60. BEGINNING COUNT-DOWN.

IT'S ALMOST TIME.
READY TO GO, TŌTA?
YEAH.
GRIMP

KURŌ-MARU!
YEAH.
JACOBS LADDER PROJECT
KARIN-SEMPAI!
YES, I'M READY.
JACOBS LADDER PROJECT
HONO-KA!
AYE, SIR!
ISANA!
JACOBS LADDER PROJECT
Y-YES, SIR!
JINBEI-SAN!
YEAH.
JŪZŌ-SEMPAI!
NOD

THREE.
LET'S GO!!
TWO.
ONE.

LAUNCH!!

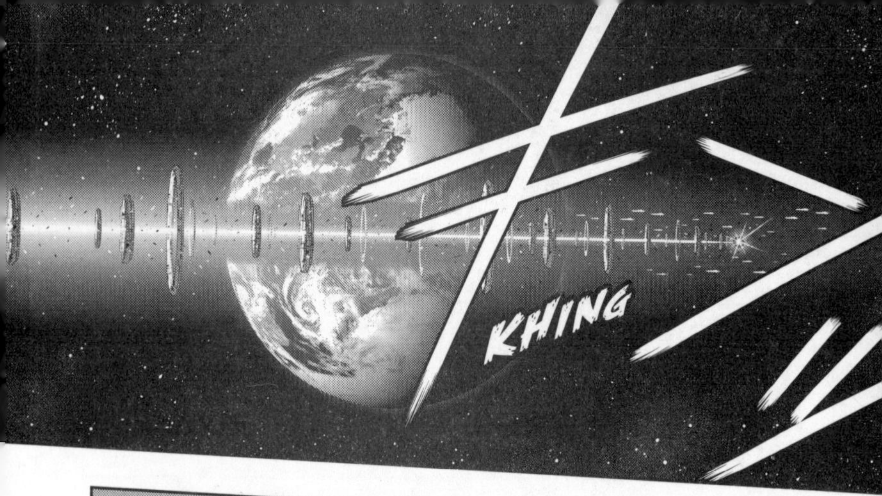
KHING

OOOHH

THMP THMP THMP

HERE IT IS!
I FOUND IT!
THMP THMP
AND ONCE AGAIN, IT'S CONSPICU-OUSLY HIDDEN IN A BOOK...
IT'S THE KEY! OKAY...
HUH?

DO YOU THINK TŌTA'S ARRIVING AT PLUTO RIGHT ABOUT NOW?
YEAH. IT'S BEEN JUST ABOUT THAT LONG...
HM?
THE KEY FITS, BUT THE BOOK WON'T OPEN...
HMMM, PERHAPS...
THIS IS A TYPE OF LOCK THAT WILL REQUIRE TŌTA-SAMA'S MAGIC.
OH!
ALL THE WAY ON PLUTO?
GUESS WE'LL HAVE TO SEND IT TO HIM THEN.
Mihashira East

WHAT.. IS THAT?

W...
WAIT, WAIT, WAIT.
WHAT IS THAT ...?

IT'S WAY TOO BIG.
MAHORA HOME
THIS BUILDING, 2F
御柱東通り
Mihasira higashi St.

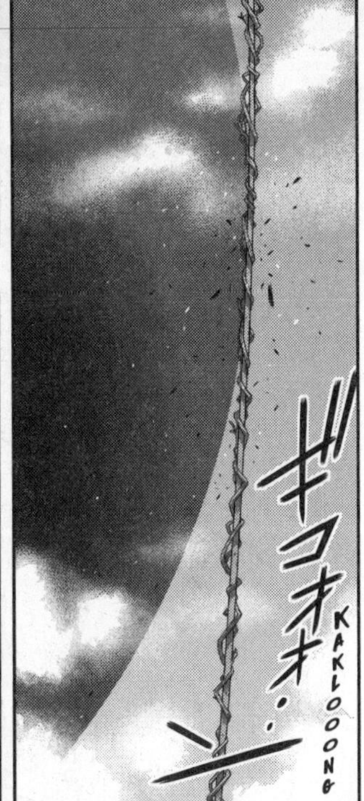
KAKLOOOONG

WAIT A–

WAAAAHH!

BOOM
A-BOOM
ZH ZH ZH

IMPOSSIBLE!
WHAT IS THAT THING?! WE DIDN'T EVEN SEE IT COMING!
A GIANT MASS HAS MATERIALIZED IN THE AIRSPACE ABOVE JAPAN! IT'S SURPASSED THE ROCHE LIMIT!
DIAMETER: 1,208KM, WEIGHT: 1.52×10^{21}KG, AVERAGE DENSITY 1.63G/CM^{3}.

ALL THE SAME TRICS AS PLUTO'S MOON HARON!!
BOOM
BOOM
BOOM
BOOM
BOOM

BOOM
BOOM
BOOM
BOOM
BOOM

BOOM
BOOM
HOW COULD THEY MOVE SOMETHING THAT BIG OVER SUCH A LONG DISTANCE?!
WE ARE CURRENTLY RUNNING ANALYSES ON ITS MARKINGS!
COMMANDER FATE! SOMETHING IS HAPPEN-ING!
19 SMALLER OBJECTS HAVE SPLIT OFF FROM THE BODY WE BELIEVE TO BE CHARON!
Charon?
Earth
AND BY SMALLER OBJECTS, I MEAN THEY HAVE A DIAMETER OF 10KM!
THEY ARE EACH ON COURSE TO COLLIDE WITH THE CAPITALS OF VARIOUS NATIONS!
GRR...
!!
HOW IS OUR PLUTO TEAM DOING?!
CHARON ...?

CHAK
PLUTO'S SURFACE
CENTRAL SPUTNIK PLANITIA

ZSHHHHHH
WHERE ARE WE?!
WE LANDED ON THE GROUND!
ZSH
OUR ARRIVAL COORDINATES WERE SUPPOSED TO BE IN PLUTO'S ORBIT...
WE WERE SUPPOSED TO STAY IN ORBIT AND OBSERVE CONDITIONS ON THE SURFACE UNTIL WE FOUND THE OPTIMAL POSITION AND TIMING TO MAKE LANDING...
LOOKS LIKE THERE WAS SOME KIND OF INTERFERENCE WHEN WE WARPED OUT.
INTERFERENCE ?!
A- ANOTHER THING...

I DON'T KNOW WHAT THIS MEANS.
BUT IF THIS IS PLUTO, THEN THE COORDINATES AREN'T QUITE RIGHT!
SOMETHING HAPPENED TO ITS GRAVITY...
PLUTO'S MOON—CHARON IS GONE...?!
THE MOON IS GONE?
HOW DOES THAT HAPPEN...?
UH...
THESE READINGS... I'M PICKING UP MULTIPLE LARGE MAGIC SOURCES ALL OVER THIS REGION!

HNGH!
ZA-ZOOM

KER-PHOOM
THAT'S...
IALDA'S BLACK MUD AND TENTACLES!
ZA-ZOOM

UH-OH...

I THINK...

IT'S A TRAP !!

IT'S A TRAP!!
STAGE 186: GENGORŌ'S WORLD LINE
BA'AL'S ELITE FOUR, EH?!!
UQ HOLDER, FULL COMBAT MODE!!
OKAY! I'LL TAKE THE ONES IN THE MIDDLE!
ZWAH
I GOT THIS!!
BAM
THAT'S SO CUTE, TŌTA-KUN.
ZWOM

HNGH...
YOU... GRAND-MA...
ASUNA-SAN...!
MINISTRA MAGI ASUNA
DIDN'T YOU KNOW?
I'M ON THE OTHER TEAM NOW.

FWOOSH
FWOH

ZSH

I'M SURE LETTING US ASSIMILATE ASUNA-SAN 45 YEARS AGO...
WAS YOUR DESPERATE ATTEMPT TO GET THE UPPER HAND, BUT IT WAS A MISTAKE.
OOHH

OOHH
ASUNA-SAN HAS THE WHITE OF MARS, THE POWER TO NULLIFY ALL FORMS OF MAGIC.
ADD TO THAT MY ORBIS SENSUALIUM PICTUS AND NODOKA'S MIND-READING,
AND NOW WE CAN EASILY DEFEAT ANY IMMORTAL.

?!

ZAM

WHAT I MEAN TO SAY IS...
...WE CAN ANALYZE YOUR IMMORTALITY'S MAGIC
AND CANCEL IT.

TŌTA-KUN!
!!

WHAT...
I CAN'T REGENERATE...
NO—AM I REALLY...?!

NOW THEN.
LET'S PUT AN END TO THIS.
VOHM
VARÝTITAS PHAKÓS. (GRAVITY MIRROR.)
"ASUNA-SAN."

TO ÁTOMO
STON
KATHRÉFTI.
(PERSON FROM
THE MIRROR)

SLASH
TMP

CLANG

PATTER
!!

THEY CAN CANCEL IMMORTALITY? THAT'S... NOT GOOD!
I DIDN'T EXPECT THIS TO BE EASY.
BUT... THIS IS TOO MUCH...

THEY'RE GOING TO BEAT US...!
IT'S ALL OVER!

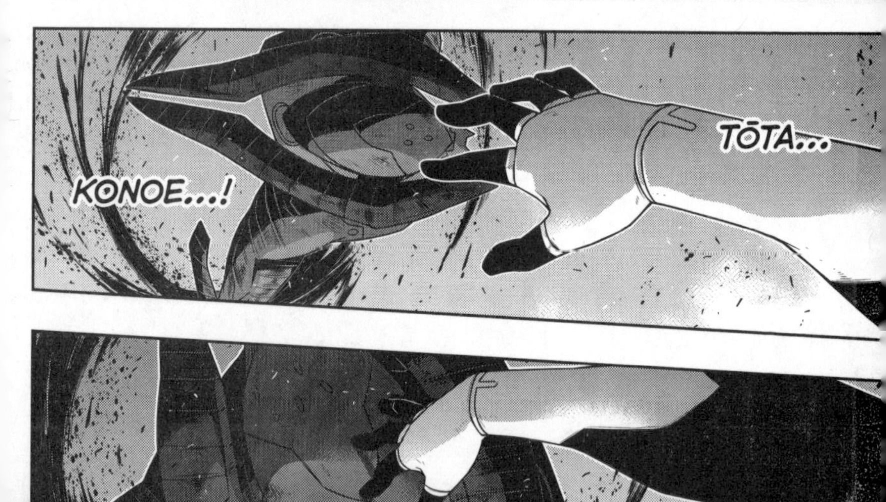
TŌTA...
KONOE...!

ブツンッ
CLICK
ピッ
PKT
パラ
PATTER
パラ
PATTER
FIP
FIP
FIP
TEP
タタ
TEP
TEP
タタ
TEP
TMP
タ―ン。
GASP

HA-
H
O
O
O
O
O

HNGH ?!

WHOOSH
SKREEEE
SKRG
GRG
GRG

WATCH OUT, KID!
YOU WANNA GET RUN OVER?!

WHA ...
HONNNK
オォォ..ン
WHAT ...?
WHERE ...
...AM I?

WH...
WHERE'S TŌTA-KUN? AND THE REST OF THE TEAM?
WHOOSH
WHOOSH
WHAT HAPPENED TO PLUTO? AND YUKIHIME-SAMA?!
REALTY
RUGAL

IS THIS A DREAM?
NO, WAS THAT A DREAM?
WAS IT ALL ...?

THMP
THMP
DON'T TELL ME...
WHAT I MEAN TO SAY IS WE CAN ANALYZE YOUR IMMORTALITY'S MAGIC...
...AND CANCEL IT.
THMP

NO...
THMP
THMP
THMP
THMP

TOKYO, 2021
INSIDE A CONVENIENCE STORE
IT'S 2021 ...
THERE'S NO DENYING IT.
THE YEAR WHEN THE INFECTION COMMONLY KNOWN AS THE NOVEL CORONA-VIRUS
HAS SPREAD ACROSS THE WORLD.
AKAMATSU TIMES
20%OFF
Q-EATS
30%off
20%OFF
...
AM I BACK HERE, IN THE WORLD I LIVED IN BEFORE I WAS IMMORTAL...
...BECAUSE THEY CANCELED MY IMMORTALITY?

THE YEAR WHEN SEEING PEOPLE IN MASKS BECAME THE NORM.
THAT YEAR.

THEN WHAT ABOUT THE OTHER WORLD?
WHAT HAPPENED THERE? WHEN I WAS DEFEATED WITH THE REST OF THE UQ NUMBERS...WERE FATE AND THE TEAM STILL ON EARTH STRONG ENOUGH TO RESIST THEIR FORCES?
OR...

...WAS IT THE END OF THE WORLD?
YO, GENGORŌ.
GASP

WHAT ARE YOU DOING STANDING AROUND HERE?
TOWARD THE FUTURE
NABA
old fashion
BEST

HUH ...? WHA-
YOU... ARE...?

HEY, THAT HURTS. SO WHAT? YOU GO UP A SCHOOL YEAR AND INSTANTLY FORGET THE NAMES OF ALL YOUR FORMER CLASSMATES?
BAM

WHAA ?

UH...

OH, NO. SORRY. NAKA-YAMA, RIGHT?
I WAS A LITTLE OUT OF IT.
YEAH, I COULD TELL. YOU WERE LOOKING REALLY UNSTEADY. I WAS SERIOUSLY WORRIED.

YOU MAKE SURE TO GET HOME OKAY.

...
SO...WHAT ACTUALLY HAPPENED?

WAS ALL OF THAT REAL?
THUD
A WORLD WHERE MAGIC EXISTS? IMMORTALS?
THAT'S COMPLETELY ABSURD.
BOOM

IT WAS JUST A DAY-DREAM... AN ESCAPIST FANTASY I HAD IN THE MOMENTS BEFORE THAT TRUCK ALMOST HIT ME.
JUST A DREAM. ...A LONG, LONG DREAM.

...
GASP
WHAT HAPPENED TO MY PARENTS, AND MY SISTER AGEHA? WHAT HAPPENED TO ME THAT DAY?

...?
status
BLINK
BLINK

...?

IS THIS ...?

BEEP

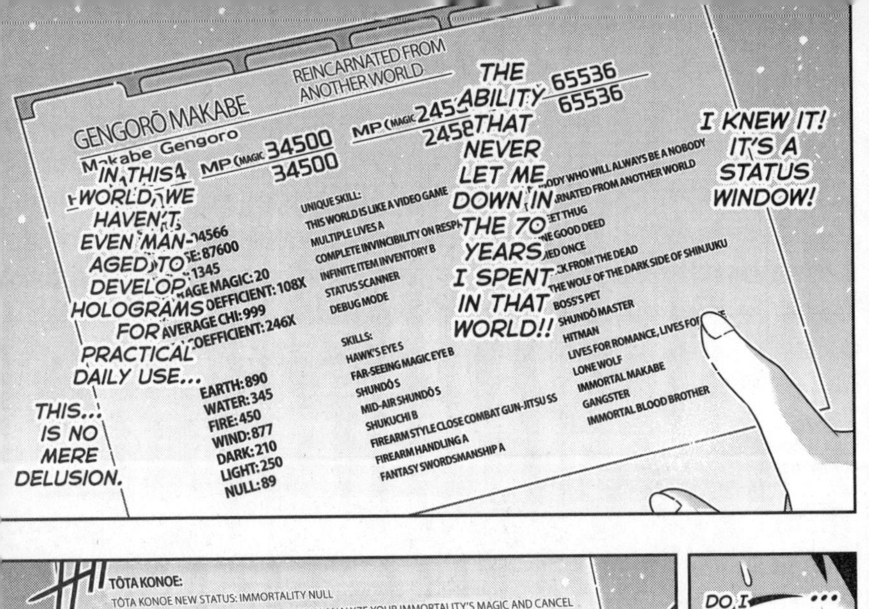
GENGORŌ MAKABE
REINCARNATED FROM ANOTHER WORLD
34500
34500
65536
65536
UNIQUE SKILL:
THIS WORLD IS LIKE A VIDEO GAME
MULTIPLE LIVES A
INFINITE ITEM INVENTORY B
STATUS SCANNER
DEBUG MODE
AVERAGE CHI: 999
SKILLS:
HAWK'S EYES
FAR-SEEING MAGIC EYE B
SHUNDŌ S
MID-AIR SHUNDŌ S
SHUKUCHI B
FIREARM STYLE CLOSE COMBAT GUN-JITSU SS
FIREARM HANDLING A
FANTASY SWORDSMANSHIP A
EARTH: 890
WATER: 345
FIRE: 450
WIND: 877
DARK: 210
LIGHT: 250
NULL: 89
BOSS'S PET
SHUNDŌ MASTER
HITMAN
LONE WOLF
IMMORTAL MAKABE
GANGSTER
IMMORTAL BLOOD BROTHER
I KNEW IT! IT'S A STATUS WINDOW!
THE ABILITY THAT NEVER LET ME DOWN IN THE 70 YEARS I SPENT IN THAT WORLD!!
IN THIS WORLD, WE HAVEN'T EVEN MANAGED TO DEVELOP HOLOGRAMS FOR PRACTICAL DAILY USE...
THIS... IS NO MERE DELUSION.

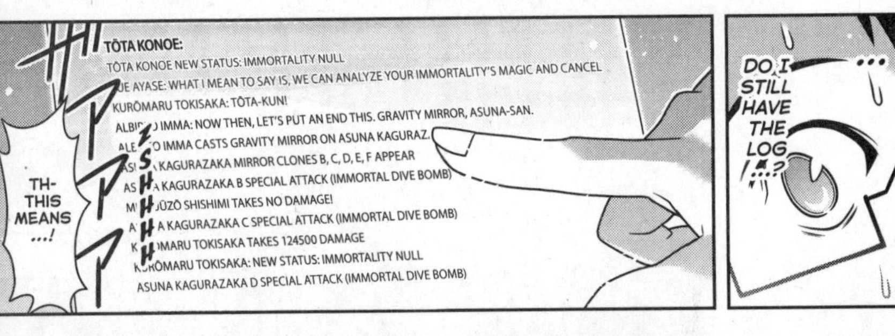
DO I STILL HAVE THE LOG...?
TŌTA KONOE:
TŌTA KONOE NEW STATUS: IMMORTALITY NULL
KURŌMARU TOKISAKA: TŌTA-KUN!
ASUNA KAGURAZAKA D SPECIAL ATTACK (IMMORTAL DIVE BOMB)
TH-THIS MEANS...!

I HAVE A PERFECT RECORD OF EVERY ATTACK USED IN THAT INSTANT BY THE ENEMIES ASUNA KAGURAZAKA, YUE AYASE, NODOKA MIYAZAKI, AND ALBIREO IMMA—INCLUDING HOW IT WAS EXECUTED, HOW IT WORKS, THE THEORY BEHIND IT, AND THE STEPS TO ACCOMPLISHING IT.
...PAI.
NOT ONLY THAT, BUT THIS EVEN TELLS ME HOW AND WHY I CAME BACK TO THIS WORLD.
IF I STUDY THIS LOG...
GENGORŌ-SEMPAI.
PAI-SEM.

COULD YOU TELL US...
...WHERE WE ARE?
HUH ...?
REALTY
WHOA, WHAT THE—?!
TŌ—WHAT?! T-TŌTA... KUN?
KUN?
WAIT.
HUH?
WHAT... WHAT ARE YOU DOING HERE?!
YOU'VE REALLY SHRUNK, GENGORŌ.
JŪZŌ...
IT WASN'T A DREAM...

CHATTER
ワイ
ワイ
CHATTER
Donny's
SO YOU'RE SAYING...
THEY CANCELED YOUR IMMORTALITY, AND AS A RESULT...
...YOU WERE SENT BACK TO THE WORLD YOU CAME FROM.
AND FOR WHATEVER REASON, WE WERE BROUGHT HERE WITH YOU?

YES.

YOU'RE PRACTICALLY THE SAME HEIGHT AS ME IN THIS WORLD.
I WAS IN MY 2ND YEAR OF JR. HIGH BACK THEN.

I WASN'T VERY TALL YET.

HEH HEH...
WHAT, JŪZŌ?

YOU'VE BEEN STRIPPED OF YOUR USUAL MASK, AND I'M FINALLY SEEING THE REAL YOU.
IT'S NOT BAD.
HMPH...

HEH HEH. BUT HEY.
WHAT, TŌTA?

SIIIGH...
SO... YEAH.
WHAT DO WE DO NOW?
HMMM...

THEY TOTALLY DESTROYED US.

YEAH.
COMPLETELY AND UTTERLY.

SHE STILL LOOKS LIKE OUR FRIENDLY ASUNA-SAN, BUT SHE IS RUTHLESS.
THAT'S HOW IALDA'S SPELL WORKS.
I CAN'T BELIEVE THEY COULD NULLIFY OUR IMMORTALITY...

I MEAN, GRANDPA'S FRIENDS WERE A BUNCH OF MONSTERS.

...STILL.
I DON'T KNOW IF THIS IS LUCK OR WHAT...
...BUT THE THREE OF US WHO GOT DRAGGED HERE WHEN I WAS MADE MORTAL ARE STILL ALIVE.
AND IF WE LOOK OVER THE LOG FROM MY STATUS SCREEN,
WE CAN ANALYZE EVERY DETAIL OF WHAT HAPPENED IN THAT MOMENT.

SO NOW...IF WE CAN JUST GET BACK TO THAT EXACT PLACE AND TIME...
...WE STILL HAVE A CHANCE TO FIGHT BACK.

GET BACK, HUH?
IF WE CAN GET BACK.
HMMM ...

ANYWAY, LET ME SEE THIS "LOG" OF YOURS.
ALL RIGHT.
CAN OTHER PEOPLE SEE IT...?

...I SEE. INTERESTING.

THANKS TO WHAT HAPPENED, I LEARNED A LITTLE ABOUT HOW EXACTLY MY IMMORTALITY WORKS.
WOW.

YEAH.

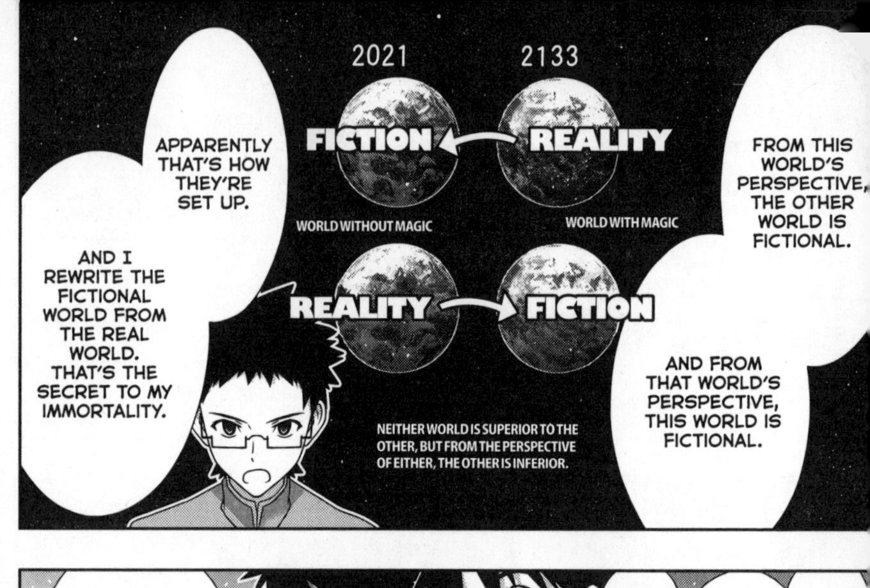
2021
2133
FICTION
REALITY
WORLD WITHOUT MAGIC
WORLD WITH MAGIC
REALITY
FICTION
NEITHER WORLD IS SUPERIOR TO THE OTHER, BUT FROM THE PERSPECTIVE OF EITHER, THE OTHER IS INFERIOR.
FROM THIS WORLD'S PERSPECTIVE, THE OTHER WORLD IS FICTIONAL.
AND FROM THAT WORLD'S PERSPECTIVE, THIS WORLD IS FICTIONAL.
APPARENTLY THAT'S HOW THEY'RE SET UP.
AND I REWRITE THE FICTIONAL WORLD FROM THE REAL WORLD. THAT'S THE SECRET TO MY IMMORTALITY.

HM?
WHAT DO YOU MEAN?
FICTION ...?
THEN IT'S NOT MERELY TRAVEL BETWEEN ALTERNATE DIMENSIONS.

RIGHT. THAT'S WHY YOU'RE BOTH HERE IN ONE PIECE,
EVEN AFTER THEY CANCELED YOUR IMMORTALITY AND CUT YOU UP.
I...
I GET IT?
BY ALL RIGHTS, NEITHER OF YOU SHOULD EXIST IN THIS WORLD.
SO WHERE DID THE BODIES YOU'RE NOW INHABITING COME FROM?

NO...
NO, I DON'T GET IT.
UH... WELL.
THEY'RE TEMPORARY BODIES MADE FROM, LIKE, SOME REALLY STRONG MAGICAL POWER?
THERE'S NO MAGICAL POWER OR ANY WAY TO USE IT IN THIS WORLD.

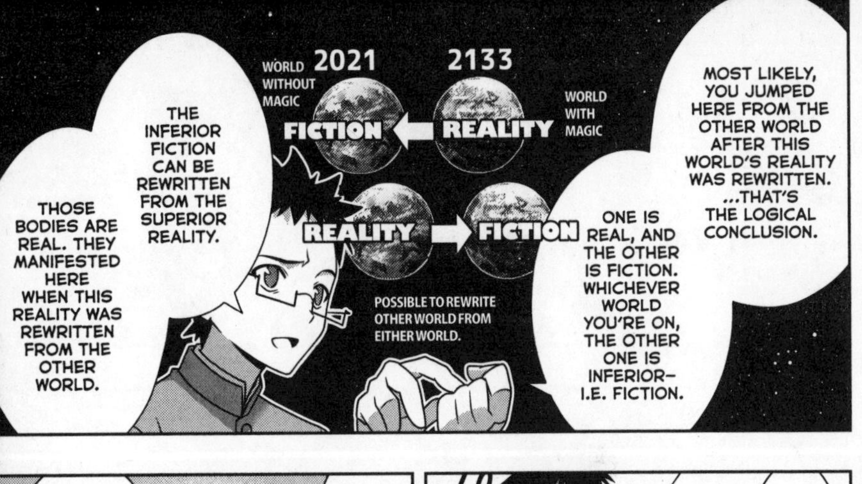
MOST LIKELY, YOU JUMPED HERE FROM THE OTHER WORLD AFTER THIS WORLD'S REALITY WAS REWRITTEN. ...THAT'S THE LOGICAL CONCLUSION.
ONE IS REAL, AND THE OTHER IS FICTION. WHICHEVER WORLD YOU'RE ON, THE OTHER ONE IS INFERIOR– I.E. FICTION.
2021
WORLD WITHOUT MAGIC
2133
WORLD WITH MAGIC
FICTION
REALITY
REALITY
FICTION
POSSIBLE TO REWRITE OTHER WORLD FROM EITHER WORLD.
THE INFERIOR FICTION CAN BE REWRITTEN FROM THE SUPERIOR REALITY.
THOSE BODIES ARE REAL. THEY MANIFESTED HERE WHEN THIS REALITY WAS REWRITTEN FROM THE OTHER WORLD.

UH-HUH.
SLICE
WHAT ARE YOU DOING, JŪZŌ-SEMPAI?
THE CUT ISN'T HEALING.
...THEN THAT BODY IS A MORTAL ONE.

HUH ...?
SO YOU'RE SAYING IF I DIE IN THIS BODY, IT'S ALL OVER?
THAT WOULD BE THE CASE.
UHHH, HRRRM-MM...?

GAAAAHH!! I REALLY JUST DON'T GET IT! IT'S WAY TOO MARVELOUS AND MYSTICAL FOR ME, SEMPAI!
BUT IT SOUNDS COOL!
THE IDEA OF BEING IMMORTAL WAS COMPLETELY ABSURD TO BEGIN WITH.
IN THIS WORLD, MAGIC AND IMMORTALITY ONLY EXIST IN FICTION.
PS5
HMM?

OH, COME ON. ARE YOU STARTING TO TALK ABOUT US LIKE WE'RE FAKES AGAIN, SEMPAI?
NO, NO. I TOLD YOU, REMEMBER? YOUR WORLD WAS REAL.
FROM THAT WORLD'S PERSPECTIVE, *THIS* ONE IS FICTION.
HNNG-HRRRM.
THIS IS HARD.

IT DOESN'T MATTER HOW IT WORKS. THE POINT IS,
IF WE PLAY OUR CARDS RIGHT, WE MAY BE ABLE TO REWRITE A FEW THINGS IN THE OTHER WORLD WHEN WE GO BACK.
!
WHAT...? SERIOUSLY?

SO WE CAN REWRITE THE OTHER WORLD SO IALDA IS JUST GONE...?
YEAH, I'M NOT SURE WE CAN PULL OFF A CHEAT OF THAT CALIBER.
BUT WE MIGHT BE ABLE TO ERASE ASUNA KAGURAZAKA'S IMMORTAL-KILLING MOVE.
OHO.
OOOOH!

MOMO
...FIG-URES.
AGAIN, THAT'S *IF* WE CAN GET BACK...
RIGHT...
HMMM...
どーん
DU-DUUUN
I GUESS WE SHOULD GO GET SOME REST...
YEAH, BUT WE HAVE NOWHERE TO GO.
AND NO MONEY.
...

I...
I'M HOME.
OH, GENGORŌ. WHERE HAVE YOU BEEN?
I TOLD YOU TO CALL WHEN YOU'RE GOING TO BE OUT LATE...
OH, YOU BROUGHT FRIENDS?
M...
MOM...
MM ...
AND DAD...
SNIFF
じわ
IT'S BEEN 73 YEARS... DAMN IT.

IS SOMETHING WRONG?
HI! THANKS FOR HAVING US!
N-NO.
MY, YOU'RE A TALL BOY!
HAVE YOU BOYS HAD DINNER?
WE HAVE SOME CURRY LEFT.
TH-THEY'RE FINE, MOM!
YOU DON'T HAVE TO FEED US!

DID I HEAR CURRY? I'D LOVE SOME!
WOULD YOU? HO HO HO.
HEY, TŌTA! DO YOU UNDERSTAND THAT WE ARE...

WHAT'S YOUR PROBLEM, SEMPAI?
YOU HAVEN'T HAD YOUR MOM'S COOKING IN FOREVER.
YOU SHOULD GET SOME NOW WHEN YOU HAVE THE CHANCE.
MRK...

GORO-KUN!
GORO-KUUUN!
PATTER
PATTER
PATTER

!

GORO-KUUUN!
GORO-KUN, YOU'RE HOME!!
Ageha
REMEMBER YOUR PROMISE, GORO-KUN! ARE YOU GONNA KEEP IT?!
NEXT SUNDAY! YOU PROMISED!!
HUH ...?
WHAT... WHAT DID I PROMISE AGAIN?
WHAT ?!
UUUUGH! MY SCHOOL SPORTS DAY! SCHOOL! SPORTS! DAY!!
UH... OH...!
RIGHT... SPORTS DAY...
OF COURSE I REMEMBER. NOTHING CAN KEEP ME AWAY, AGEHA.
YAY!
NOW, AGEHA. IT'S BEDTIME. YOU SHOULDN'T BE UP THIS LATE.
NO! I'M NOT DONE TALKING TO GORO-KUN!
YOU'RE JUST TRYING TO STAY OUT OF BED.
...
SO.
READY FOR SOME CURRY?

THE SMELL OF THIS ROOM BRINGS BACK SO MANY MEMORIES...
THINGS I'D FORGOTTEN FOR SO LONG.

MOM... DAD...
THEY HAVEN'T CHANGED A BIT.
THAT'S GOOD.

AND AGEHA...
SHE'S ALIVE AND RUNNING AROUND, THE LITTLE TWERP...
WAS SHE ALWAYS THAT CUTE?

I CAN'T BELIEVE IT...
I ACTUALLY GOT TO SEE THEM AGAIN.
I ALWAYS THOUGHT... EVEN IF I LIVED FOREVER, I WOULD NEVER LIVE TO SEE THIS HAPPEN.

I LIKE THIS PLACE.
LIKE...

EVEN WITHOUT MAGIC,
THE WORLD JUST KEEPS ON TURNING.

AND I THINK THAT'S OKAY.

YEAH, BUT WITH NO MAGIC, THE IDEA OF BUILDING THAT ORBITAL ELEVATOR YOU LOVE SO MUCH IS STILL JUST A DREAM WITHIN A DREAM.
YEAH, WELL...

I MEAN, WHEN YOU GET DOWN TO IT, HAPPINESS IS DIFFERENT FOR EVERYBODY.
LIKE, THAT WOULDN'T AFFECT HOW YOU LIVE YOUR LIFE.
HMPH.
BUT THIS WORLD HAS ITS PROBLEMS, TOO, LIKE THE NOVEL VIRUS.
EVEN WITHOUT THAT, THE ECONOMY IS SHRINKING, THIS COUNTRY IS IN DECLINE. IT CAN'T GIVE YOUNG PEOPLE ANY HOPE FOR THEIR FUTURE.
THAT HOPELESSNESS IS WHY I...

STILL, THERE'S SOMETHING IN THE AIR HERE.
AND I KINDA LIKE IT.

...

THEN DO YOU WANT TO STAY? JUST LIVE HERE?
TŌTA KONOE.

IF YOU STAY, YOU CAN LIVE OUT YOUR LIFE AND DIE LIKE A NORMAL MORTAL.

NAH... I MEAN, THE PEOPLE I CARE ABOUT ARE IN THE OTHER WORLD.
TRUE.

THE PEACE HERE IS NOT THE PEACE WE ARE MEANT TO PROTECT.
YEAH ...

WAIT...
BUT...

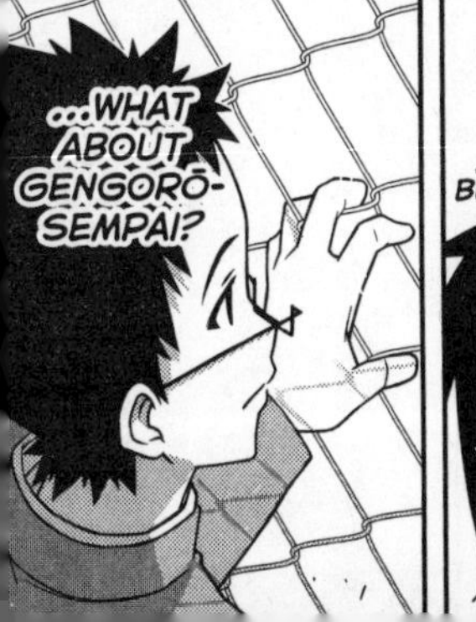
...WHAT ABOUT GENGORŌ-SEMPAI?

AFTER LOOKING OVER THE LOG, I'M CONVINCED.

IF WE SUFFER IMMEDIATE DEATH IN THIS WORLD, WE CAN GO BACK TO THE SAME TIME IN THE OTHER WORLD.
BUT THERE'S A TIME LIMIT. FIVE DAYS.

AND I ALREADY HAVE THE PERFECT STRATEGY FOR A COUNTER-ATTACK.

IT'S ENOUGH TO MAKE ME THINK I WAS REBORN IN YOUR WORLD PRECISELY FOR THIS MOMENT.

MAYBE YOU WERE... WITHOUT YOUR UNIQUE SKILL, GENGORŌ-SEMPAI, WE COULD HAVE ALL BEEN WIPED OUT.

THEN PERHAPS I'LL USE THE FIVE DAYS WE HAVE LEFT TO STUDY THIS LOG FURTHER.

...
BUT SEMPAI.
I WONDER IF MAYBE YOU SHOULDN'T GO BACK?
I MEAN...YOUR DAD AND YOUR MOM ARE HERE IN THIS WORLD... AND YOUR FRIENDS...AND YOUR LITTLE SISTER.
IT'S TRUE. I GOT ALONG FINE WITH MY PARENTS.
I WASN'T ESPECIALLY WORRIED ABOUT MY FUTURE EDUCATION. I DON'T HAVE A GIRLFRIEND, I HAVE TYPICAL FRIENDSHIPS...
IF I WENT TO THE OTHER WORLD, THEY WOULD PROBABLY TREAT IT LIKE A STRANGE DISAPPEARANCE.
THEN YOU'LL-!
NO.
I'M STILL GOING.
...

I'M PRETTY SURE I WAS REINCARNATED IN YOUR WORLD...
...BECAUSE I'M WORTHLESS AS A HUMAN BEING.

...WORTH-LESS?

YES.

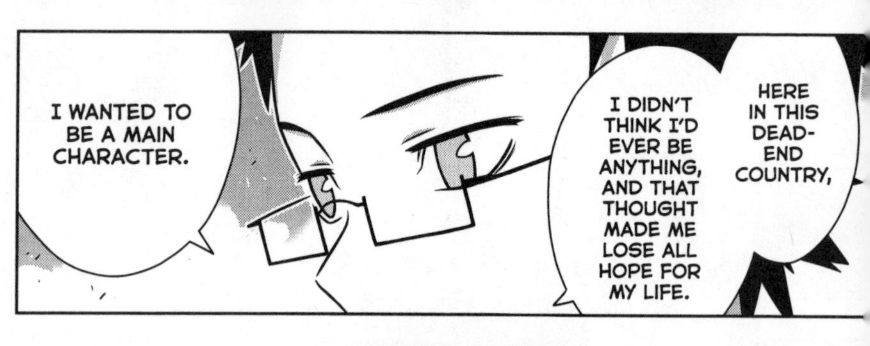
HERE IN THIS DEAD-END COUNTRY,
I DIDN'T THINK I'D EVER BE ANYTHING, AND THAT THOUGHT MADE ME LOSE ALL HOPE FOR MY LIFE.
I WANTED TO BE A MAIN CHARACTER.

I WANTED TO BE THE MOST POWERFUL VERSION OF MYSELF, AND HAVE BIG, HEROIC EXPLOITS.
AND SOME GOD OR AUTHOR OUT THERE DEIGNED TO GRANT MY SHALLOW WISH.

I WAS HERE, SURROUNDED BY SO MANY BLESSINGS...
I WAS SUCH A FOOL.

ZZzZ

WHAM
WHAM

HEY.
LET'S GO, TŌTA.
NGAH?

DON'T WAKE HIM.
I WON'T.

...

WE'RE GOING BACK TODAY.
WHAT?
I TOLD GENGORŌ THAT I'D TAKE YOU FOR SOME SIGHTSEEING AROUND TOKYO.

BUT WE HAVE UNTIL TO-MORROW, DON'T WE...?
I LIED.
SO THAT WE COULD GO AND LEAVE HIM HERE.

...

RIGHT, TODAY IS SUPPOSED TO BE AGEHA-CHAN'S SPORTS DAY.
AND HE'S NOT THE SORT OF MAN WHO WOULD BREAK A PROMISE TO HIS SISTER.

SURELY A PROMISE TO HIS SISTER IS MUCH MORE IMPORTANT...
...THAN BRINGING PEACE TO SOME UNKNOWN FOREIGN WORLD.

BUT JŪZŌ-SEMPAI.
WE NEED GENGORŌ-SEMPAI TO REWRITE THE OTHER WORLD'S REALITY. WE CAN'T FIGHT AGAINST GRANDMA ASUNA WITHOUT HIM.
IS THIS REALLY A GOOD IDEA?

I'VE LOOKED AT THE LOG, AND I'VE LEARNED THE TRICK TO HER IMMORTAL-KILLING MOVE.
AS LONG AS I KNOW HOW IT WORKS, I CAN CUT IT DOWN.
OH...
WE CAN FIGHT BACK WITHOUT HIM. WE CAN TURN THIS AROUND.
HUH.
COOL.
SOUNDS GOOD TO ME.
GRIN
GRIN

WHAT DO YOU MEAN, "SOUNDS GOOD"?
IDIOT.
G...
GENGORŌ-SEMPAI...?
YOU'RE SO STUPID.
DON'T YOU GET IT?
WITHOUT ME, YOU CAN'T ALTER THIS WORLD'S REALITY.
AND THAT MEANS, WHEN YOU FALL TO YOUR DEATHS, YOUR MANGLED CORPSES WILL STAY RIGHT WHERE THEY ARE.
SELF-CENSORED
IMAGINE IF TWO FRIENDS WHO STAYED WITH ME FOR FIVE DAYS SUDDENLY KILLED THEMSELVES.
OUBLE SUICIDE?
MY LIFE, MY LIVELIHOOD, AND MY FAMILY'S LIVES WOULD BE COMPLETELY RUINED.
THINK FOR A SECOND. YOU, TOO, JŪZŌ.
URK...
BUT GENGORŌ-SEMPAI.

DON'T YOU THINK YOU SHOULD STAY AND LIVE YOUR LIFE HERE...?
THIS IS YOUR CHANCE TO START OVER.

...

I ALREADY KEPT MY PROMISE TO WATCH MY SISTER'S SPORTS DAY.

BE-SIDES.
YOUR WORLD IS MY WORLD NOW, TOO.
I OWE YUKIHIME-SAMA AND JINBEI-SAN.

AND I LOVED SOMEONE WHO LOVED THAT WORLD.
THERE ARE PEOPLE I CARE ABOUT THERE.
YOU CAN'T EXPECT ME TO FORGET ALL THAT AND GO BACK TO MY OLD LIFE.

...
GEN-GORŌ-SEMPAI.
I HAVE TO FINISH WHAT I STARTED.

BE-SIDES...
I MAY NOT HAVE HAD A PURPOSE BEFORE,
BUT I HAVE ONE NOW.
!

POOF
ポン
ワイ
WALLA
ワイ
WALLA
ポポン
PA-POOF

LOOK, GORO-KUN!
I GOT SECOND PLACE!
3-2
MAKABE

YEAH.
YOU DID GOOD.

ARE YOU PROUD OF ME? ARE YOU PROUD?
3-2 MAKABE
VERY PROUD.

AGEHA.

ぎゅっ
HUG
EEK!

YOU'RE A GOOD GIRL.
PET
なでなで
PET
EH HEH HEH.

ZSH

OH, GENGORŌ. LEAVING ALREADY?
MOM.
ワーワー
WAAH WAAH
Musashino Municipal Kichijoji Elementary School

UH, YEAH.
I GOT A THING I HAVE TO TAKE CARE OF WITH MY FRIENDS.

OH.

WELL ...

TAKE GOOD CARE OF YOURSELF.

WHOOSH
SHE KNOWS...?

AND MAKE SURE TO BE BACK IN TIME FOR DINNER.

OKAY.
I PROM-ISE.

I'M GONNA SAVE THE WORLD
AND COME BACK TO MY FAMILY!!
HEH.
NICE, SEMPAI.
I'LL DO EVERYTHING I CAN TO HELP.
WELL, OKAY THEN!
LET'S GO!
DASH
YEAH!!

WHOA!
WHOOSH
AA
AA
AA
AA

AH!
THIS IS A NEW FEELING FOR ME.
I'M SCARED!!
THIS IS A MORTAL BODY!
I'M AN ORDINARY HUMAN IN A WORLD WITH NO MAGIC AND NO CHI ENERGY!
WHAT IF I KEEP FALLING AND GO SPLAT... AND THAT'S IT?
...
WELL, IF IT HAPPENS, THEN I GUESS THAT'S THAT!
STAGE 187: COSMO ENTELEKHEIA

SPLAT

GASP
ACOBS
ADDER
ROJECT

TŌTA-KUN!
!!

NOW THEN.
LET'S PUT AN END TO THIS.
WHOM
VARÝTITAS PHAKOS. (GRAVITY MIRROR.)
ASUNA-SAN.

TO ÁTOMO STON KATHRÉFTI. (PERSON FROM THE MIRROR)

FLASH

I SEE.
SO YOU'VE COME BACK.

BRAVO.
I'D EXPECT NOTHING LESS OF NEGI-SENSEI'S GRAND-SON.

YOU'RE PRETTY GOOD...
...TŌTA-KUN.

THE REST...
...IS UP TO YOU.
SHHH

YEAH. I GOT THIS.
THANKS, GRAND-MA.

SEND-
ING CON-
DENSED
REPORT!!
IALDA'S
APOSTLES,
ASUNA
KAGURAZAKA,
NODOKA
MIYAZAKI,
YUE AYASE.
WE REFLECTED
THE IMMORTALITY
NULLIFICATION
BACK AT THEM
AND FORCED
THEM OUT OF
THE BATTLE!

WHAT?
WAIT A...
WHAT?
WHEN
DID
YOU--?
IT'S A
LONG
STORY!!

SWOOSH

ALRIGHTY
THEN.

HNNGH
...
OHO.
NOT
BAD,
KID.

ZAAA
LET'S GO, TEAM!!
WE'RE GONNA KICK SOME IALDA-APOSTLE BUTT!
TIME TO FIGHT BACK!!
THE BOMBINGS FROM OUR ORBITAL FLEET ARE HAVING NO EFFECT!
THE WHITE TITANS ARE STILL ADVANCING!!

THEY APPEAR TO HAVE DEPLOYED COMPOSITE DEFENSIVE FIELDS USING A POWERFUL COMBINATION OF MAGIC SHIELDS AND SPACE-TIME DISTORTION!
I WANT A DETAILED ANALYSIS OF THEIR DEFENSES AS SOON AS YOU CAN GET IT!!
IF THE TARGETS ADVANCE ANY FARTHER, THEY'LL ENTER DENSELY POPULATED AREAS! IT WILL BE HARD TO LAUNCH A LARGE-SCALE ATTACK!!
GRR!

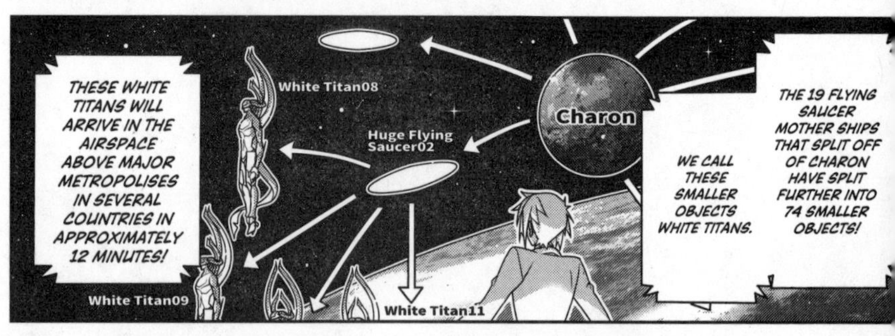
THE 19 FLYING SAUCER MOTHER SHIPS THAT SPLIT OFF OF CHARON HAVE SPLIT FURTHER INTO 74 SMALLER OBJECTS!
WE CALL THESE SMALLER OBJECTS WHITE TITANS.
Charon
White Titan08
Huge Flying Saucer02
White Titan09
White Titan11
THESE WHITE TITANS WILL ARRIVE IN THE AIRSPACE ABOVE MAJOR METROPOLISES IN SEVERAL COUNTRIES IN APPROXIMATELY 12 MINUTES!

THEY EASILY BROKE THROUGH THE NATIONS' BORDER DEFENSES! ONLY THREE COUNTRIES MANAGED TO REPULSE THEM!
White Titan
1200m
AND THERE ARE MORE THAN 70 OF THEM...
THEIR DEFENSIVE FIELDS AND WEAPONS ARE SEVERAL GENERATIONS AHEAD OF OUR MOST ADVANCED ARMS TECHNOLOGY!
EACH TITAN IS 1200 METERS IN HEIGHT!
THEY'RE STRATEGIC WEAPONS FROM ANCIENT VENUS. THE TECHNOLOGY IS ON A COMPLETELY DIFFERENT LEVEL.
YOU CAN'T FIGHT THEM.
NIKI-TIS.

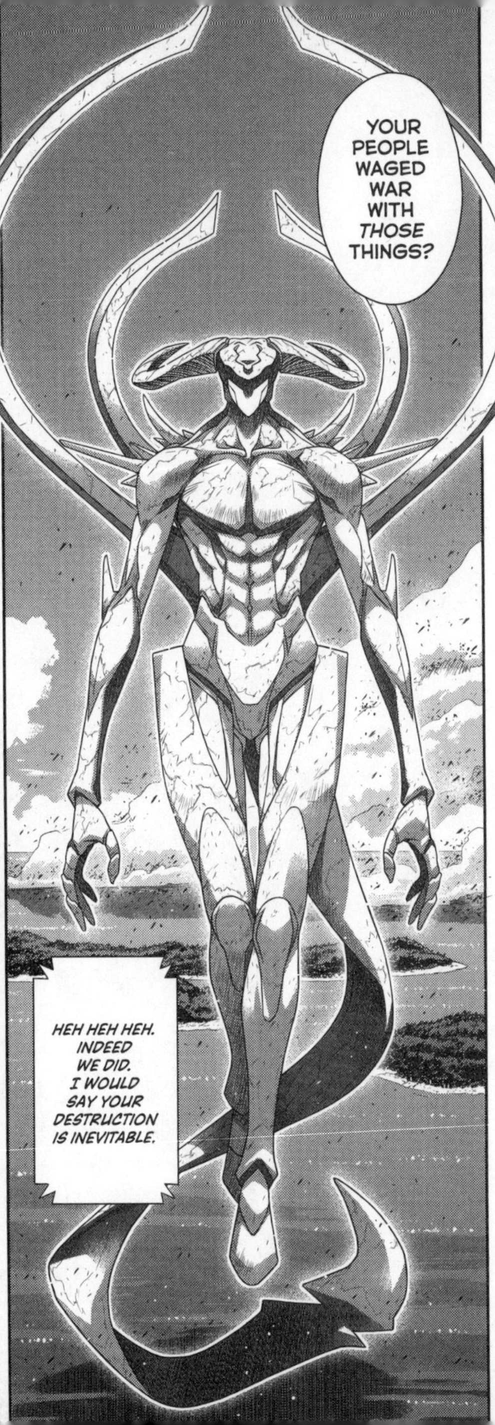
YOUR PEOPLE WAGED WAR WITH *THOSE* THINGS?
HEH HEH HEH. INDEED WE DID. I WOULD SAY YOUR DESTRUCTION IS INEVITABLE.

BUT WHY? IF SHE CAN ACTIVATE A MASSIVE SPELL FROM PLUTO THAT WOULD COVER THE ENTIRE SOLAR SYSTEM, THERE SHOULD BE NO NEED TO RESORT TO THESE TACTICS...

THIS IS NOT HOW IALDA WORKS.
AND THAT MEANS...

HEH, HEH HEH. YOU PLAYED RIGHT INTO MY HANDS, YOU FOOLS.

VNN...
!
SOMEONE HAS IN-FILTRATED OUR OPTIC COMM LINE!

THIS IS YOUR DOING?!
PURE-BLOOD BA'AL!

YES, IT IS.
WE HAVE NOT YET COMPLETED THE REQUIREMENTS FOR ACTIVATING IALDA'S COSMO ENTELEKHEIA SPELL.
OOOHH
HER PERFECT WORLD SPELL WOULD FELL THE ENTIRE SOLAR REGION, BUT IN ORDER TO CAST IT,
THERE ARE TROUBLESOME STEPS TO FOLLOW AND RESTRICTIONS THAT MUST BE OBEYED, REQUIRING THE AVATAR EVANGELINE TO SUCCUMB AND ALLOW US TO COLLECT THE DISPERSED ACTIVATION KEYS.
ON THE OTHER HAND...
OOOHH
...IF I PERSONALLY INVITE EACH INDIVIDUAL MEMBER OF THE HUMAN RACE
INTO A COSMO ENTELEKHEIA OF MY OWN MAKING, THE RESTRICTIONS NO LONGER APPLY.
PERSONALLY?
YES.
OOOHH
I LOVE THE HUMAN RACE SO DEARLY THAT I WILL PRESENT EACH OF ITS MEMBERS ...
...WITH A HEARTFELT INVITATION TO A PERFECT WORLD.

OVER THE LAST FORTY-FIVE YEARS, WHILE YOU TWIDDLED YOUR THUMBS, HELPLESS TO ACCOMPLISH ANYTHING,
I HAVE BEEN HARD AT WORK, FORMU-LATING MY PLAN.
I WILL LEVEL THE EARTH'S ENTIRE SURFACE, AND I WON'T NEED THREE DAYS TO DO IT.
ZH
ZH
ZH
ZH
ZH
BA'AL... WHY ARE YOU SO DETERMINED TO DO THIS?
FOR FOUR HUNDRED... NO, TWELVE THOUSAND YEARS, I HAVE BEEN WATCHING, AND YOU NEVER CHANGE.
AT THE BEGINNING OF THE 20TH CENTURY, THE HABER-BOSCH PROCESS GAVE YOU THE ABILITY TO CAPTURE ATMOSPHERIC NITROGEN, ALLOWING YOU TO PRODUCE FOOD IN MUCH GREATER QUANTITIES. THUS YOU ESCAPED THE MALTHUSIAN TRAP AND MANAGED TO INCREASE IN NUMBERS.
BUT THEN WHAT?

ZA-ZHOOM
OOOHH
OOOOHH
WAAAH
AAAAH
KHEEE
THE CHAOS AND CALAMITIES OF THE 20TH CENTURY TOOK A MORE INSIDIOUS SHAPE. HUMANITY WAS DIVIDED.
ALL OF THE WEALTH GOES TO THE FORTUNATE FEW, WHILE THE UNFORTUNATE ARE CAST ASIDE, NEVER TO SEE A BETTER LIFE.
KHEEE
OOOOOHH
KH-
KH-
KH-
KH-
KHEE
WAAAH
INEQUALITY IS BECOMING A PERMANENT FIXTURE OF SOCIETY.
KHEEEEEEEEEE
INDIVIDUAL MISERY AND SUFFERING CONTINUE TO RISE UNCHECKED.
WALLA
WALLA

SO.
IT WOULD BE BETTER FOR YOU ALL TO TAKE A BREAK.
DON'T YOU AGREE?
BA'AL...!
DETECTING A CHANGE IN THE WHITE TITANS! THEIR HEADS ARE RADIATING LIGHT!
WE IMMORTALS WILL TAKE ON THE ROLE OF THE SOLAR SYSTEM'S SPIRITUAL LEADERS!!
WHOOSH
IF ANY OUTSIDE THREAT APPROACHES FROM THE FAR REACHES OF SPACE, *WE* WILL STRIKE THEM DOWN!!
KHEEE
EEEEEEE
HHHH
OHHH
WH-WHAT THE--? THAT GIANT'S HEAD LIT UP!
WAAAH
WHAT IS GOING ON?
HEY, SHOULDN'T WE RUN...?
ALL THE WEAK ONES OF YOUR WORLD WILL BE TAKEN TO A GLORIOUS AFTERNOON NAP!!
REST, ALL PEOPLE! REST IN PEACE!!
WHAT IS IT GOING TO DO?
AAAAHH
UNKNOWN. BUT THE HEAT LEVEL IS LOW. ITS OBJECTIVE IS NOT TO DESTROY.
SO WE'LL BE OKAY?
IT'S HUGE!
NO...
WAAH
KH KH KH KH KH KH
BA'AL!!
TŌTA!

BOOM

WAAAAH
AAAAAH

THEY'RE LIGHTING UP AGAIN! WE ASSUME THIS IS A SECOND WAVE!!
EVERYONE IN THE TITANS' LINE OF FIRE IS DISINTEGRATING INTO WHITE ASH!!
THE FIRST ATTACK ALONE HAS REDUCED OVER 7 MILLION TO DUST!
IF WE DON'T DO SOMETHING...

BOOOM

ZSHH

OHHH
HH
THIS WILL BE THE END OF HUMAN HISTORY!!
OOH
OOOOO
OOO
OHHH
BOOM
KA-BOOM
BA-BOOM
ZWAH
RRR-AAH!

SLASH!
HA HA!
FWOOM
KHI-
GA-
KHI-
KHING
SLICE

SWOOSH
WHOOSH
SHINMEI SCHOOL SECRET FINISHING TECHNIQUE!
SHIN RAIKŌKEN!!
FLAMMEUM GLADIUM
ATQUE VERSATILEM!!
BOOM
BOOM
KABOOM
NEXT !!

ZHNG
ZHNG
KA-ZHNG
POW
POW
POW
CHAK
BANG
BANG
OHH

PURPLE LIGHTNING STARRY FROST!
KHING
BOOM

ZWOH

WITHOUT GRAND-MA AROUND,
YOU GUYS...

HNNGH!
...ARE NOTHING.

YOU'RE NO MATCH FOR US!
KONOE SCHOOL BLOOD MANIPU-LATION!
BOOOOM

GWAA-AAAHH!
BOOM
SWISH

BLOOD CATARACT!
BA-
BA-
BA-

GAH!
NGH!
SLASH

HRRGH!
WA-WHOOSH

SKSSH
GRR!
ROOM
DAMN YOU, TŌTA KONOE!
DAMN YOU, UQ HOLDER!
ISH
YOU GUYS AREN'T WORTH OUR TIME!!
BRING US YOUR LEADER!! WE WANNA SEE THE LAST BOSS!!
KON...E...
!!
CAN YOU HEAR ME, TŌTA KONOE?!
FATE?!!
I GOT THROUGH! I'M USING AN EXPERIMENTAL INSTANT INTERPLANETARY COMM LINK!
WHAT? WHOA! YOU'RE SENDING THE SIGNAL AT, LIKE, SUPER LIGHT SPEED...
FOCUS, TŌTA KONOE!
THIS IS A TRAP!
YEAH, WE FIGURED.
LISTEN.
IALDA BAOTH CAN'T ACTIVATE COSMO ENTELEKHEIA FROM PLUTO YET!
THERE IS NO POINT IN YOUR BEING THERE.
!
SERIOUSLY?
!
!

LIVE
BUT PLUTO'S MOON CHARON HAS TELEPORTED AND IS FLOATING ABOVE EARTH.
WHAT'S WORSE, ANCIENT SUPER-WEAPONS WE BELIEVE THE PUREBLOOD BA'AL RECOVERED FROM VENUS, AS WELL AS THE FLEET HE USED TO RECOVER THEM, ARE LAUNCHING A LARGE-SCALE ATTACK.
White Tit
THEY'VE BEGUN CASTING HIS CHEAP COPY OF COSMO ENTELEKHEIA OVER EVERY INCH OF THE EARTH, STARTING IN THE MOST DENSELY POPULATED AREAS.
LIVE
e Titan08
Charon
Huge Flying Saucer02
ite Titan11
THE CASUALTIES HAVE ALREADY SURPASSED 50 MILLION. IF WE DON'T STOP THEM, THEY'LL HAVE COVERED THE ENTIRE PLANET IN LESS THAN FOUR DAYS!!

SO YOU'RE SAYING A MAJOR CRISIS HIT EARTH WHILE WE WERE GONE?!
THAT CREEP, BA'AL!!
OUR TEAM HAS PINPOINTED BA'AL'S CURRENT LOCATION AT THE CENTER OF THE ENORMOUS RUINS AT THE NORTH POLE OF CHARON, WHICH IS NOW SITUATED IN THE AIRSPACE ABOVE AMANO-MIHASHIRA CITY.
I'M PUTTING TOGETHER A STRIKE TEAM OF THE MOST ELITE FIGHTERS CURRENTLY AVAILABLE IN THE SOLAR SYSTEM, BUT CONSIDERING THIS WILL BE ANTI-IMMORTAL AND ANTI-PUREBLOOD WARFARE, I WANT TO LEAVE NOTHING TO CHANCE.
I NEED ALL OF YOU!!
I'LL BE USING A FORCED DEGENERATION OF THE DISTORTION FIELD TO BRING YOU BACK IN 20 SECONDS!
!
CAN YOU BE READY?!
YOU CAN DO THAT?
I'M IN! DO WHAT YOU HAVE TO!
IT IS A RATHER DRASTIC MOVE. I DON'T KNOW WHAT WILL HAPPEN AND I CAN'T GUARANTEE...
THAT'S OKAY! WE'LL BE FINE!

THEN GET READY!
EVERYONE GATHER AROUND KONOE!
GOT IT!
5
4
3
2
YES, SIR!
SKSH
TMP
TSH

1
0
BA-BLAM
BA-BOOM
KA-KHING

...
HUSH
...HM?

DWAAA-AHH?!
BOOOOM

FATE!
NOTH-ING'S HAPPEN-ING!

WHAT'S WRONG?
S-SOME-ONE'S HACKED THE SYSTEM!

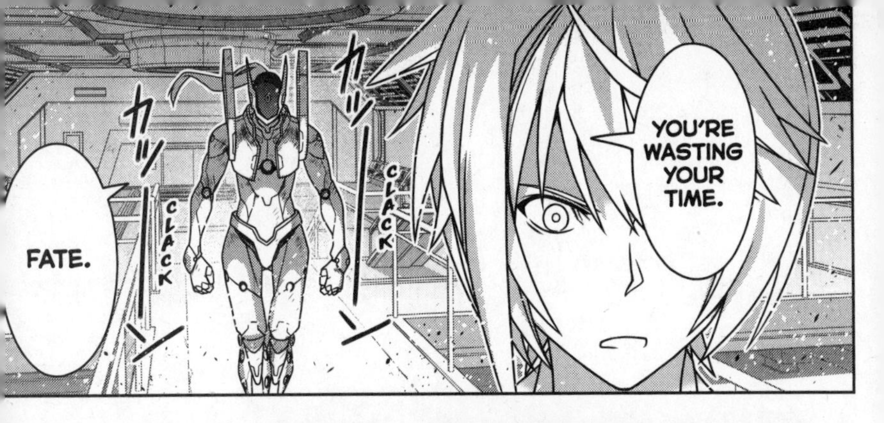
YOU'RE WASTING YOUR TIME.
CLACK
CLACK
FATE.

CLACK
THAT ALLIED SPACE FLEET IS CURRENTLY MANKIND'S BEST HOPE IN THIS WAR, RIGHT? WELL, I JUST TOOK OVER ITS SYSTEMS.

IKKŪ AMEYA ...
ZSH
!
IKKŪ-SEMPAI ?!
WE'VE FINALLY REACHED THE END-GAME.

YOU CAN'T USE THE INTERNET ANYMORE, AND IT LOOKS LIKE YOU MANAGED, SOMEHOW OR OTHER, TO MAINTAIN THIS LARGE FLEET WITH THAT PRIMITIVE DIRECT OPTICAL COMMUNICATION.
BUT TOO BAD, SO SAD.
FRANKLY, WITH MY SKILLS, I COULD HAVE TAKEN IT OVER WHENEVER I WANTED TO.
AND I'M GOING TO LET THE NUMBERS WASTE AWAY ON PLUTO.
...!
FATE, CAN YOU HEAR ME?
SANTA! CALL SANTA!
HE'S THE ONLY ONE WHO CAN FIGHT IKKŪ-SEMPAI!
SANTA IS...

GOODBYE, TŌTA-KUN. GOODBYE, UQ HOLDER.
I WILL DEFEAT YOU AND LIVE FOR ETERNITY.

CLICK

GRR!

TŌTA-KUN, UP THERE!
!

?!
ZA-SHOOM
HNGH!
SMACK
HNNGH!
ZOOSH
NGH!
RRRGH ...
OUR TRUE MASTER HAS ARRIVED.
YOU WILL BOW YOUR HEADS IN HER PRESENCE.
AGH ...
MRSH
MRSH
THIS... INTENSE PRESSURE ...!!
GSH
GSH
...NGH!!

OOOH
GSH
GSH

THE MAGE OF THE BEGINNING.
THE LIFEMAKER OF THE RED STAR.
TMP
OOOH

SHE WHO WILL BRING PEACE TO ALL HUMAN RACES.
A SAVIOR SPRUNG FROM HUMANKIND.

IALDA BAOTH
ARCHON.
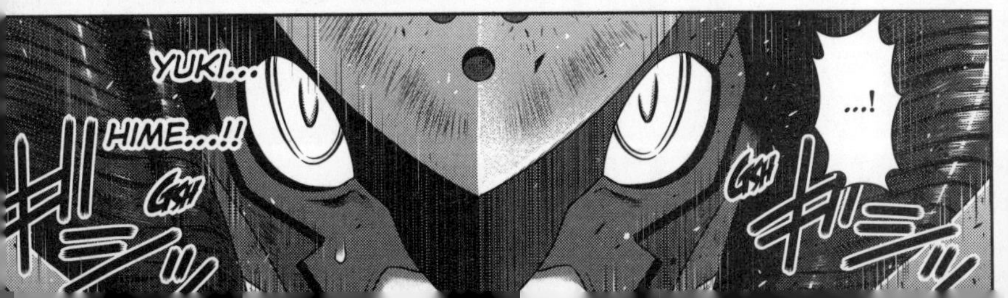
...!
YUKI...
HIME...!!
GASH
GASH

YUKIHIME ...!
NO, SHE'S EVA IALDA NOW.
OUR ULTIMATE ENEMY.

オォォォォォ
AND A WOMAN I AM DUTY-BOUND TO SAVE.
SHE'S MY...

BOW YOUR HEAD.
I WAS GONNA SAY THAT...
TŌTA KONOE.

ZA-ZOOM

HNGH!
MRSH
MRSH

SHE'S NOT.
SHE'S... STILL YUKIHIME.

NO... ...SHE'S NOT.

IF SHE CAN'T ACTIVATE COSMO ENTELE-KHEIA YET,
THAT MEANS YUKIHIME HASN'T GIVEN IN!
GSH
GSH

ISN'T THAT RIGHT...!
GRG
GRG
GRG

RRRAAAAAHI!
MR-ZHRNGH

KA-SNAP
AAAHH!

WHAT?!

AMAZING! TŌTA-KUN... YOU BROKE THROUGH IALDA'S PRESSURE!

!
I CAN MOVE!

TŌTA-KUN!
BAM

YUKI
HIME
EEEEEEEEE!

KA-
KHIIIING
HNGH!
POW
POW
AGH!
POW
AAAAAAH!
SWISH
GSH
MR
GH
HNGH!
GRAB

YUKI-HIME!!
SNAP OUT OF IT, STUPID!!

IT IS NO USE.
THIS GIRL WILL NOT AWAKEN.

I THANK YOU FOR BRINGING THE KEY TO ME.
GSH
GSH

I KNOW THAT MY CRADLE WILL HAVE NO EFFECT ON YOU.
AND SO...

I WILL SHOW YOU WHAT THIS GIRL HAS SEEN.

!!

I WILL SHOW YOU
HELL.
OH.

SLASH

THOONK
WELL DONE.
SPLASH
BUT SURELY YOU'RE AWARE, FATE,
THAT THIS ISN'T MY MAIN BODY.
GWONG

YES. MY REAL BODY IS A PUNY LITTLE OLD MAN, LYING IN A HOSPITAL BED.
MOST OF THAT OLD MAN MAY BE ON THE INTERNET, BUT MY IMMORTALITY IS STILL DEPENDENT ON HUMAN COMPUTING RESOURCES—THAT MAKES IT FAR FROM PERFECT.
I WANT TO WIN THIS BATTLE AND RESOLVE THAT ISSUE.
WITH THE DEFEAT OF HUMANKIND'S LAST FLEET, AND THE ANNIHILATION OF UQ HOLDER...
...I WILL MAKE MY IMMORTALITY COMPLETE.
...!
DAMN IT! YOU'VE HAD YOUR ENTIRE FLEET TAKEN OVER AGAIN?! YOU ARE SO INCOMPETENT!

NANAKO! IS THERE ANYTHING WE CAN DO?!
THE FIRST STEP TO A SOLUTION IS ON ITS WAY!
WHAT ?!
ARRIVING IN 5...
4...
3...
KH
2...
1...
EN
HE IS HERE.
CLAP
!

OH!
YOU'RE ...
FSHHH

COME ON, MAN. I AM SO DISAP-POINTED.
IKKŪ-SEMPAI.

HERE I THOUGHT YOU AND I WERE TWO OF A KIND, BUT BOY WAS I WRONG.
YOU'RE PATHETIC.
I HAD NO IDEA YOU WERE SO OBSESSED WITH "COMPLETE" IMMORTALITY.
WHAT... DID YOU SAY?
I *SAID* I DON'T GIVE A DAMN ABOUT IMMORTALITY.
BUT NEVER MIND THAT.
I'M GONNA BEAT YOU, YOU STUPID PHONY, GET THE **REAL** IKKŪ-SEMPAI BACK, AND RECLAIM THE INTERNET FOR HUMANITY.

I KNOW YOU WERE BEING MIND-CONTROLLED AND ALL, BUT YOU'RE SERIOUSLY GONNA HAVE TO PAY FOR TAKING THE INTERNET AWAY FROM US.
TO BE HONEST, WHETHER YOU'RE A PURE BEAN OR AN EDGELORD, WITHOUT THE INTERNET...
...THIS WORLD ...
...IS BORING AF!!
KA-
KLIIING

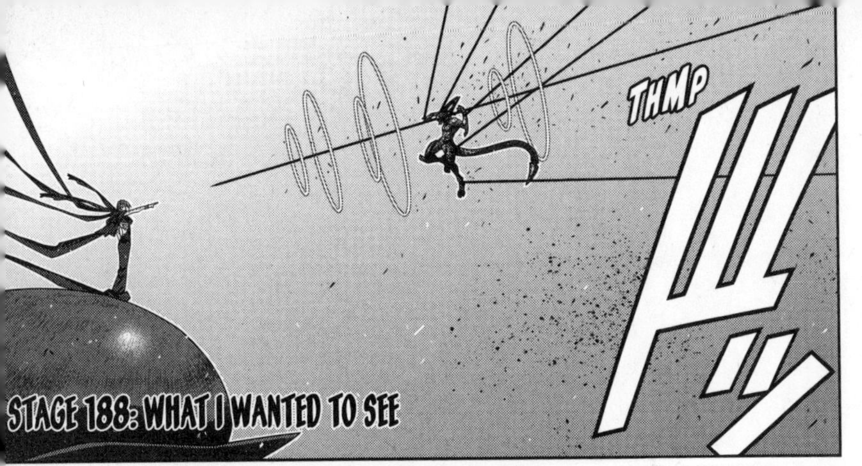
THMP
STAGE 188: WHAT I WANTED TO SEE

TŌTA-
K...

ZHOOM

SPLOOSH

HNGH...
GAH!
AAA
AAA-
GHH!
AAHH!

DU-
DUN

AGH...
WHAT... IS THIS?
WHAT AM I SEEING? IS...

IS THIS...
...THE RESONANCE?!

JUST LOOKING AT IT...
...MAKES ME FEEL LIKE MY MIND IS BEING PHYSICALLY SHAVED AWAY, ONE LAYER AT A TIME...
WHOOOM

WHAT'S HAPPENING? I'M SCARED!
I FEEL SICK!
IT'S IALDA BAOTH'S UNIQUE SKILL—INFINITE EMPATHY WITH ALL HUMANKIND!!
THIS IS WHAT IALDA HAS BEEN SEEING SINCE THE DAWN OF HISTORY.
ALL THE CRUELTY, INTENTIONAL HARM, ATROCITIES, DISCRIMINATION, UNLAWFULNESS, INJUSTICE, UNRIGHTEOUSNESS, INHUMANITY, WICKEDNESS, VULGARITY, AND BASENESS PERPETRATED THROUGHOUT HUMAN HISTORY!!

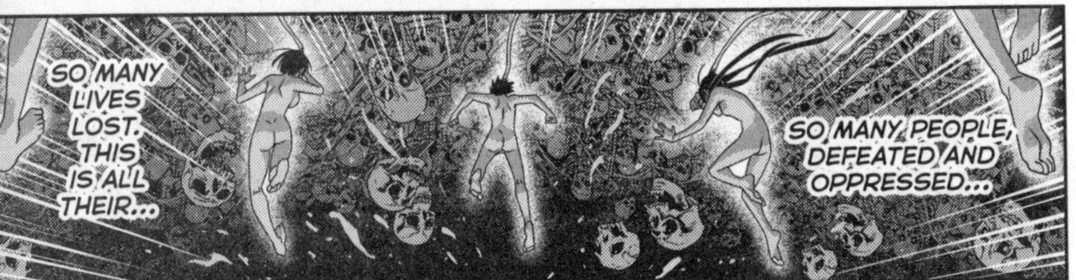
SO MANY PEOPLE, DEFEATED AND OPPRESSED...
SO MANY LIVES LOST. THIS IS ALL THEIR...

GRUDGES
LOVE-HATE
REGRET
DETESTATION
MALICE
ENVY
ENMITY
BITTERNESS
RESENTMENT
VENGE-FULNESS
ANGER
MALICE
INDIGNATION
DISCONTENT
JEALOUSY
GRIEF
LAMENTATION
HATRED
ENMITY
ABHORRENCE
CURSES
REVULSION

THROUGH THE CENTURIES I'VE WITNESSED ALL OF THIS FROM THE OUTSIDE...
BUT THIS IS WHAT WAS GOING ON INSIDE THEIR MINDS...

POW
HAVEN'T YOU LEARNED NOT TO SHOW YOUR FACE AROUND HERE?!

GET OUT!!
GO TO HELL WHERE YOU BELONG!!
DIE!!
ZHOOM
AGH!

RIIING
GOOONG
RIIING
GOOONG

LITTLE WITCH-LING!
FWAM
WHAM
VAM-PIRE!
UGH, YOU STINK!!
JINX!!

AH...
COUGH!
KA-HEGH...
YU...

WHAA
SHE'S A WITCH!
SHE'S THE ONE WHO BROUGHT THE BLACK DEATH HERE!
AAHH
HANG HER!!
NO, BURN HER!
DEATH TO THE DEVIL!
O LORD, HAVE MERCY!

POW

YUKI... HIME.

NO...
STOP!
WAAHH
RIIING
GOOONG
AAHH
YUKIHIME-SAMA, NO...!
RIIING
GOOONG

YUKI-HIME!!
DAMN IT, STOP THAT!!
YUKI-HIME-SAMA!
FWOOOM
ROO
ARR
YUKI-HIME-EEEE!
GRG
GRG
GRG
GRG
GRG
GRG
MEANWHILE, NEAR EARTH
LAGRANGE POINT 3

GRG
GRG
GRG
GRG
GRG
GRG

HRRRGH!
GRG
GRG

WHAT'S WRONG, SANTA-KUN?
DID YOU USE UP ALL YOUR BRAVADO AT THE BEGINNING OF THE FIGHT?
GRG
GRG
GRG
GRG

GRK
GRK
GRK
GRK
AGH...
AH...
GRNGH!
SA...
SHAKE
SHAKE

SANTA!
ARGH!
WHAT IS WRONG WITH YOU, SANTA? PULL YOURSELF TOGETHER!!
SHAKE
SHAKE
AUGH-GH-GH!
DAMN IT, YOU'RE A BETTER MAN THAN THAT!
OR DID I MISJUDGE YOU?!
HEEEY!
HUSH, NIKITIS-SAMA.
IF YOU CANNOT PARTICIPATE IN THE ELECTRONIC BATTLE, THEN KINDLY STAY OUT OF THE WAY.
WHAT?!
HA HA HA! YOU BEAT ME LAST TIME BECAUSE WE WERE ON YOUR HOME TURF.
BUT NOW MY COMPUTATIONAL RESOURCE...
...IS THE ENTIRE SOLAR SYSTEM!
OF COURSE, I'M NOT TAKING IT FOR FREE. I'M USING 17% OF MY ABILITIES TO SUPPORT HUMAN INFRASTRUCTURE.
IF I WERE OUT OF THE PICTURE, HUMANKIND WOULD GO BACK...WELL, I WOULDN'T SAY TO CAVEMAN DAYS, BUT AT LEAST BACK TO THE 19TH CENTURY.
FOR THE LAST 45 YEARS, AMERICA, RUSSIA, CHINA, THE EU, INDIA, INDONESIA, NIGERIA, AND OTHER ADVANCED NATIONS HAVE MANAGED TO AVOID BECOMING DEPENDENT ON ME THROUGH SOME TRULY HEART-RENDING EFFORT, BUT IT'S ONLY A MATTER OF TIME.
WHAT I'M SAYING IS, EVEN WITHOUT USING THE INTERNET, HUMANITY CANNOT LIVE WITHOUT ME.
IN A SENSE...
...I HOLD THE LIFE OF EVERY MODERN HUMAN IN MY HANDS.
YOU'RE NOT...
GRIT
...IKKŪ-SEMPAI.

WHAT?
IKKŪ-SEMPAI...
...WOULD NEVER
SAY THAT STUFF!
KRGRK
...
GRGRK
HEH...
GRGRK
HA HA!
HA HA HA HA!
AH HA HA HA HA HA HA HA!
HA HA HA HA HA HA HA HA!
...
HEH HEH HEH HEH.
AAAHH...
OH, SANTA-KUN. WHAT WOULD YOU KNOW?
LET ME TELL YOU HOW THE REAL IKKŪ TRULY FEELS.

THE REAL IKKŪ...
...DOESN'T WANT TO DIE.

WHA ...?
AFTER GROWING AND EVOLVING TO THIS SIZE AND STATURE...
...IF IKKŪ HANDS OVER THE INTERNET RESOURCES TO HUMANS, IKKŪ WOULD BE FINISHED.

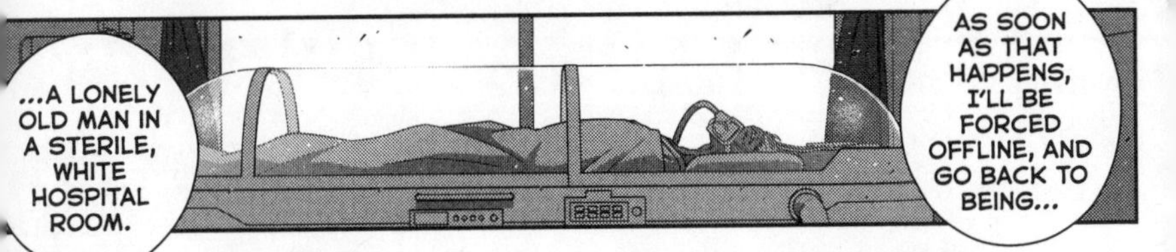
AS SOON AS THAT HAPPENS, I'LL BE FORCED OFFLINE, AND GO BACK TO BEING...
...A LONELY OLD MAN IN A STERILE, WHITE HOSPITAL ROOM.

I NEED HUMANITY'S COMPUTATIONAL RESOURCES TO SURVIVE.
I'M NOT LIKE YOU REAL IMMORTALS.
CONTROLLED BY IALDA OR NOT...
...IKKŪ AMEYA CANNOT LET YOUR SIDE WIN.

THAT'S RIGHT!
I WAS NEVER UNDER IALDA BAOTH'S CONTROL!!
I DID IT FOR MY OWN SURVIVAL!
AND I'M RISKING EVERY-THING I HAVE!
I'M PUTTING IT ALL ON THE LINE!
WHAM
TO DEFEAT YOU!!

GRG
GRG
URG!
GHAAAAAAAGH!
BUT I DON'T WANT YOU TO WORRY.
SANTA-KUN! UQ HOLDER!
GRG
GRG
GRG
GRG
WHILE HUMANKIND IS ROCKING PEACEFUL-LY IN ITS CRADLE...
...I WILL KEEP THEM PERFECTLY SAFE AS I CONTINUE TO EVOLVE.

I KNOW! FIRST, I'LL GET STARTED ON THE CONSTRUCTION OF A DYSON SPHERE!
OH, BUT THAT WILL BE TRICKY, SO I'LL TRY A RING! A RINGWORLD! WE'LL GET A HUGE AMOUNT OF LAND!
IT WILL BE A MASSIVE UNDERTAKING THAT COULD TAKE MILLENNIA!!
RING WORLD
SUN
Solar System Defense Intelligence Fleet
TO PROTECT HUMANKIND FROM OUTSIDE THREATS, WE'LL TAKE A FEW HUNDRED MILLION—NO, A FEW BILLION YEARS TO BUILD A SMART FLEET CAPABLE OF SUPER-LIGHTSPEED NAVIGATION!!
AND ONCE WE SOLVE THE SECURITY AND ENERGY PROBLEMS, WE COULD EVEN START WAKING PEOPLE UP IN STAGES.
IT'S JUST A TEMPORARY PAUSE FOR HUMANITY. WHEN IT'S OVER, THEY'LL HAVE A GREAT, BIG, BEAUTIFUL TOMORROW WAITING FOR THEM!
OF COURSE, IT WILL BE ABSOLUTELY ESSENTIAL THAT WE IMMORTALIZE THE ENTIRE SPECIES!
AFTER ALL, ALL OF MANKIND'S PROBLEMS COME FROM ITS LIMITATIONS!
DEATH FIRST OF ALL, AND THE LIMITED AMOUNT OF LAND, RESOURCES, AND ENERGY!
TWITCH
...?
HRRG
HRRG
WHAT THE...?
HNGH
HG-GNG

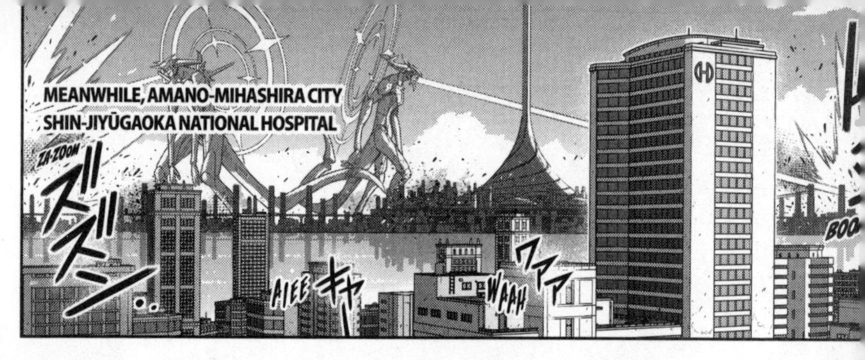
MEANWHILE, AMANO-MIHASHIRA CITY
SHIN-JIYŪGAOKA NATIONAL HOSPITAL
ZA-ZOOM
AIEE
WAAH
BOO

A-02
IKKŪ AMEYA
LONG-TERM CARE WARD

BEEP
BEEP
WAAAH
BA-BOOM

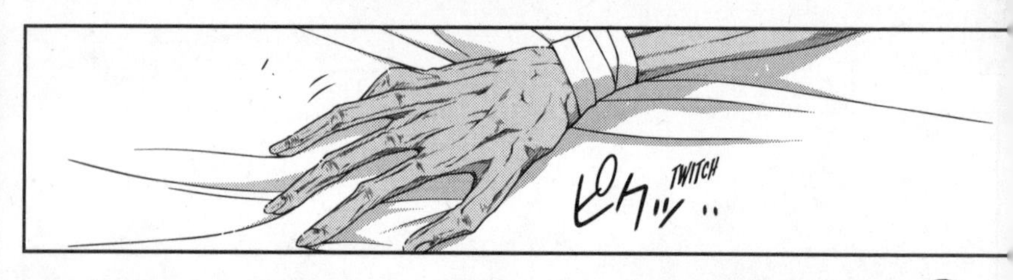
TWITCH

WHAT...
IS HAPPENING?
GSH
GRG
GRG
I'M...

HNGH
BEING...
GRN
GRN
GRN
OVER... POWERED ...?
GWAHH
SANTA!!
NICE ONE, SANTA!!
THAT'S IMPOSSIBLE! ALL YOU HAVE ARE A FEW ELECTRONIC BATTLESHIPS AND YOUR ONE AKASHIC SHIP!
I HAVE THE ENTIRE THE SOLAR SYSTEM UNDER MY CONTROL! YOU CAN'T POSSIBLY BE STRONGER THAN...
YOU...

NANAKO!
DA-
DUN
I MEAN, SEPT SHICHIJŪRŌ NANAO!!
NO...
YOU DID THIS ...?
YES, IKKŪ-SAMA.
WE HAVE BEEN MAKING PROGRESS ON A PROJECT TO RECLAIM YOU.
THE SOLAR SYSTEM STILL CONTAINS...
...ENOUGH COMPUTATIONAL RESOURCES TO SURPASS THE ACCUMULATED POWERS OF ALL YOUR ELECTRONIC CIRCUITS.

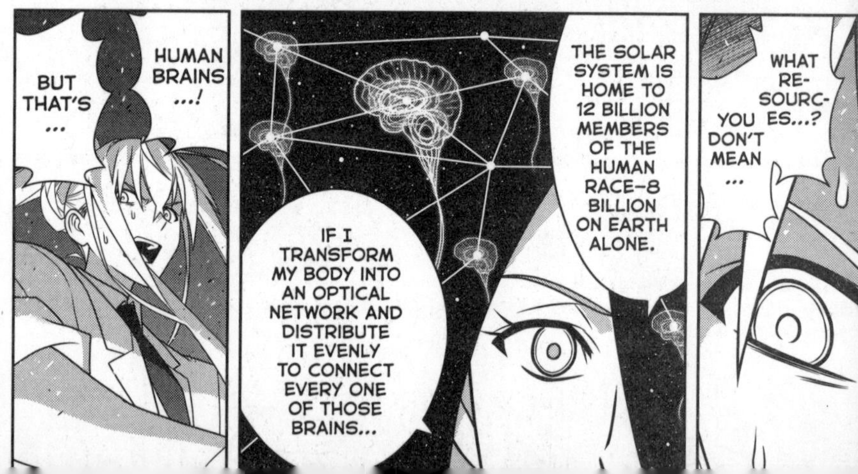
WHAT RE-SOURC-ES...?
YOU DON'T MEAN ...
THE SOLAR SYSTEM IS HOME TO 12 BILLION MEMBERS OF THE HUMAN RACE–8 BILLION ON EARTH ALONE.
IF I TRANSFORM MY BODY INTO AN OPTICAL NETWORK AND DISTRIBUTE IT EVENLY TO CONNECT EVERY ONE OF THOSE BRAINS...
HUMAN BRAINS ...!
BUT THAT'S ...

OF COURSE, I CAN ONLY TAKE UP RESIDENCE IN ALL OF HUMANITY'S BRAINSPACE FOR A FEW MINUTES AT A TIME
AND, THANKS TO BA'AL'S ATTACK, THE NUMBER OF PEOPLE HAS BEEN DIMINISHING.
NEVER-THE-LESS...
OOOHH
AT THIS MOMENT IN TIME, IKKŪ-SAMA, IT IS QUITE SUFFICIENT
TO OVERWHELM YOU.

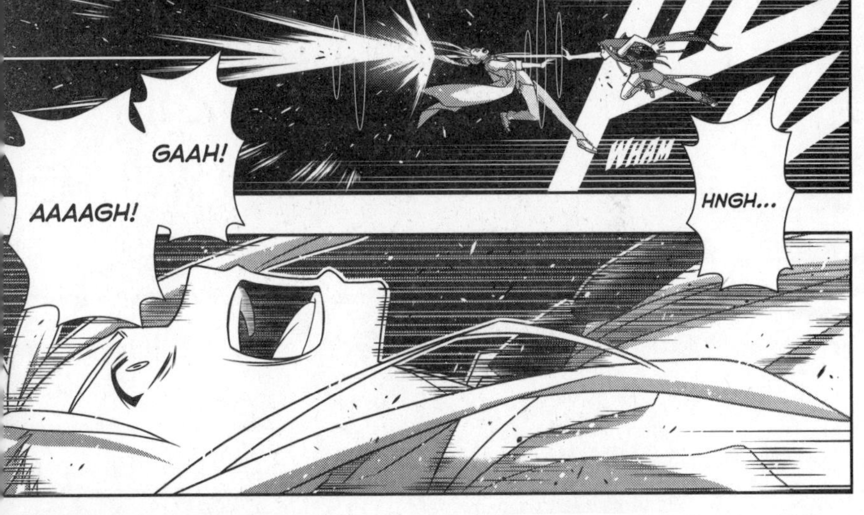
WHAM
HNGH...
GAAH!
AAAAGH!

NOW!!
SANTA-SAMA!

WHAT IS WRONG, SANTA-SAMA?
...!

I CAN'T...
I CAN'T SAVE IKKŪ-SEMPAI...!

IF I WIN THIS BATTLE...
IKKŪ-SEMPAI WILL...

THERE IT IS. THOSE EYES.
IKKŪ ALWAYS HATED THOSE EYES.

!!

YOU IMMORTALS ARE OVER-WHELMINGLY STRONG.
BUT YOU'RE SO ARROGANT, YOU HAVE TO PITY THE WEAK.

YOU COULD JUST STAY OUT OF HUMAN AFFAIRS LIKE THE MONSTERS YOU ARE, BUT YOU *HAVE TO* REACH OUT!
YOU HAVE TO START TALKING ABOUT SAVING THE WORLD!

YOU DAMN IMMOR-TALS!
YOU MAKE ME WANT TO VOMIT!!

KA-KRAK

CLAMP

SANTA !!
SANTA-SAMA!

IF YOU WANT TO HELP THE WEAK, THEN IALDA BAOTH'S PLAN AND MY PLAN ARE SO OBVIOUSLY THE RIGHT WAY TO GO!
IF YOU'RE SO TORN ABOUT IT, YOU COULD HAVE JUST MINDED YOUR OWN BUSINESS!
YOU HIGH-AND-MIGHTY IMMORTALS!
GRG
GRG
GRG
GRG
HA HA HA HA HA HA HA HA!
FWAAA
JKLJ
AH HA HA HA HA HA HA HA HA!
B-DMP
B-DMP
HA...
HUH ...?

YOU'RE RIGHT.
HNGH...
MAYBE IKKŪ-SEMPAI...
WOULD SAY SOMETHING LIKE THAT.
SCRUNCH
KA
BUT...
AT THE VERY LEAST, HE KNOWS THAT I'M ONE OF THE WEAK.
HE KNOWS THAT IT'S ALREADY OVER FOR ME.
IKKŪ-SEMPAI...
MIGHT SAY THAT STUFF.
BUT HE WOULD NEVER SAY IT TO ME.

ISN'T THAT RIGHT?
IKKŪ-SEMPAI?

GNN

YES.

I'M SORRY, SANTA-KUN.
FOR MAKING ...
YOU DO THIS...

SHOONK

THUD

IKKŪ... SEMPAI.
I...
I...

SEM ...!
ZSHHHH
WHAT I WANTED TO SEE...
...WAS HUMANS' PROG-RESS.
SHHH
I DIDN'T WANT TO DIE...
...BECAUSE I WANTED TO SEE HOW FAR THEY COULD GO.
BUT...IF I'M GOING TO BE AN OBSTACLE TO THAT PROGRESS ...
...THEN I'LL STEP OUT OF THE WAY.
BUT...
BUT...
THAT'S NOT REALLY HOW YOU FEEL, EITHER!
I...I CAN TELL!
I KNOW WHAT IT FEELS LIKE TO BE ONE OF THE WEAK! I...
HUG

SHHH
IT'S OKAY.
THANK YOU...
SANTA-KUN.

KEEP GOING.
ALL OF YOU.
ZSSHHHH

KEEP GOING.
SANTA-KUN.
SHHH

KEEP GOING...
BEEP
BEEP
BEEP
BEEP
WHOOOOSH

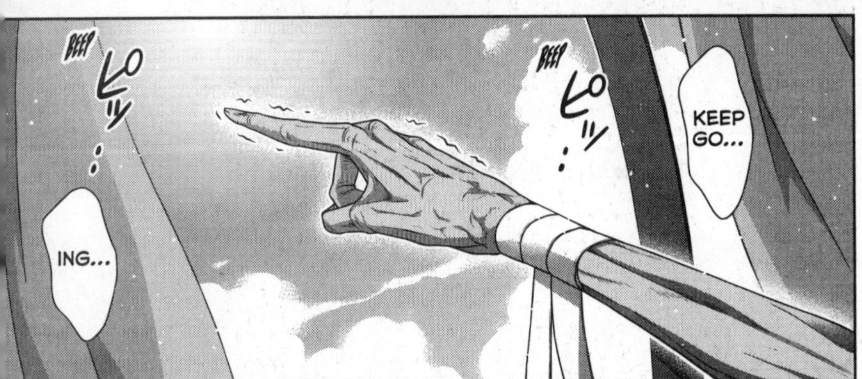
KEEP GO...
BEEP
BEEP
ING...

BEEEEEEEEEEP

CHIRP
CHIRP
TWEET
TWEET

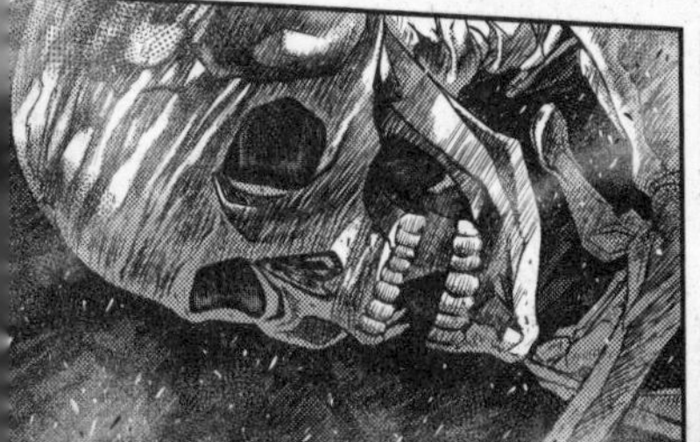

RATTLE
ガラ
ガラ
RATTLE

ZSH
ZSH

ZSH
ZSH
ZSH

ヒュオオオオオ
WHOOOOSH

ZSH
ZSH
ZSH

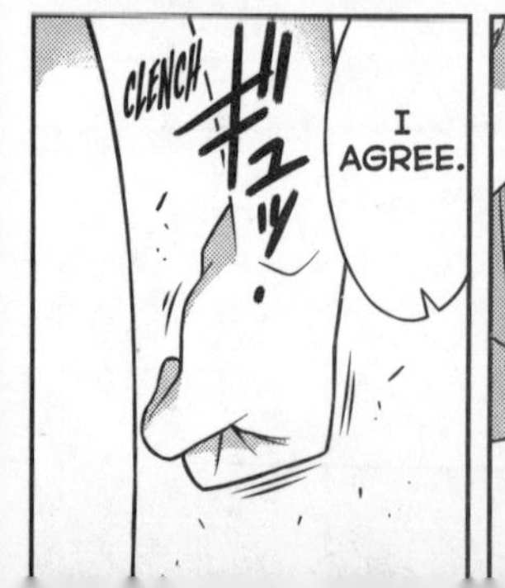
I AGREE.
CLENCH
ギュッ

IF SOMEONE FORCED ME TO SEE THIS HELL FOR THAT LONG,
I MIGHT WANT TO PUT AN END TO IT ALL, TOO.
GRR
HEH ...
PLEASE.
IF YOU WERE TO LOOK BACK AT ALL OF THE ATROCITIES COMMITTED BY THE HUMAN RACE, THIS ONE IS HARDLY WORTH MENTIONING.
ONLY A DROP IN THE OCEAN.
YOU THINK I DON'T KNOW THAT?!
IALDA !!
!!

YOU ...
GRIN
KHEEN

GSH
...!

YUKI ...
HIME ...

SHE'S PROBABLY GOING TO BE RIGHT, YOU KNOW.
AS LONG AS SHE STANDS WITH THE LOSERS.
AND THE LOSERS–
THE DEAD–NEED SOMEONE TO SPEAK ON THEIR BEHALF.

BUT...

YOU'RE GOING TO KEEP GOING FORWARD.
AREN'T YOU, TŌTA?

...!
YEAH.

GOOD.
NOW GO.
GRNK

WHAT'S HAPPENING...?!
WHOOOS
I SUSPECT...
IT'S SANTA AND NANAO'S DOING...
AND IKKŪ'S.
Y...
YUKI-HIME!
GO.
YUKI-HIME!
YUKI-HIME!
I PROMISE I'LL COME BACK FOR...!

NO...
DON'T WASTE YOUR TIME ON ME.
THERE IS NO FUTURE WITH ME.
WHA-?!
WHY WOULD YOU SAY—
TAKE THEM INTO THEIR FUTURE.
YUKI-HIME-EEE!

S...
SUC-CESS!
WE DID IT!
WHOOSH
HNGH...
WHOO HOO OOO
UQ HOLDER NUM-BERS HAVE SUCCESS-FULLY RETURNED FROM PLUTO!

NGH...
ARE WE...?
ON EARTH ...?

TŌTA KONOE.
FATE!

I'M GLAD YOU'RE ALL RIGHT.
THOUGH, NOT SURPRISINGLY, YOU DO LOOK SOMEWHAT WORSE FOR WEAR.
WHAT'S THIS? WERE YOU WORRIED ABOUT US? THAT'S SO UNLIKE YOU.
IS THE MOON GONNA FALL OUT OF THE SKY?
ONE ALREADY DID.

HUMANITY IS IN CRISIS. WE NEED YOU AND YOUR TEAM'S HELP.
I'M SORRY, BUT I'M PUTTING YOU RIGHT BACK TO WORK.

MRK ...
チラッ GLANCE

YEAH.
YOU CAN COUNT ON US.

GOOD.
FIRST, GO FOR A VITALS CHECK, EAT, TAKE A SHOWER, AND CHANGE INTO YOUR PILOT SUITS.
COME TO THE BRIDGE WHEN YOU'RE DONE.
WE HAVE TWO HOURS BEFORE THE FINAL MISSION.
OOO
TWO HOURS, HUH?
I'M SORRY, BUT WE DON'T HAVE MUCH CHOICE.

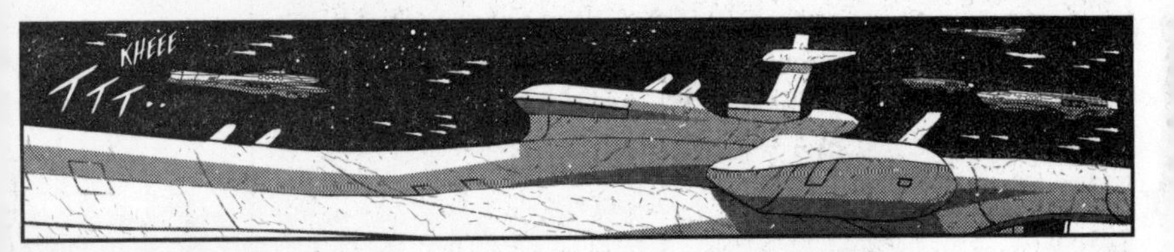
KHEEE

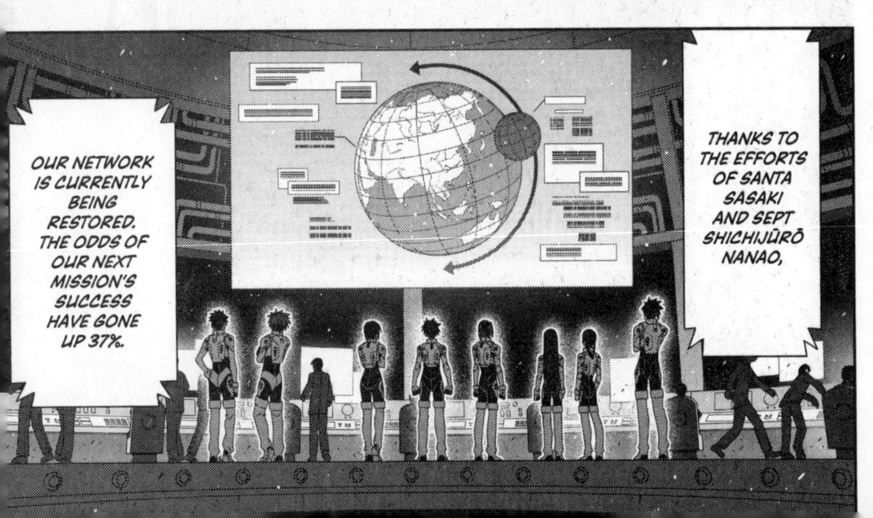
THANKS TO THE EFFORTS OF SANTA SASAKI AND SEPT SHICHIJŪRŌ NANAO,
OUR NETWORK IS CURRENTLY BEING RESTORED. THE ODDS OF OUR NEXT MISSION'S SUCCESS HAVE GONE UP 37%.

FOR REAL?
...
AND IKKŪ-SEMPAI ...?
JACOBS LADDER

UNFORTUNATELY, IKKŪ AMEYA HAS...
...!

OH... I SEE.
JACOBS LADDER

...
JACOBS

HERE IS THE RECORD OF HIS FINAL ELECTRONIC BATTLE.
SANTA-KUN SAYS HE'D LIKE YOU TO SEE IT.
...!

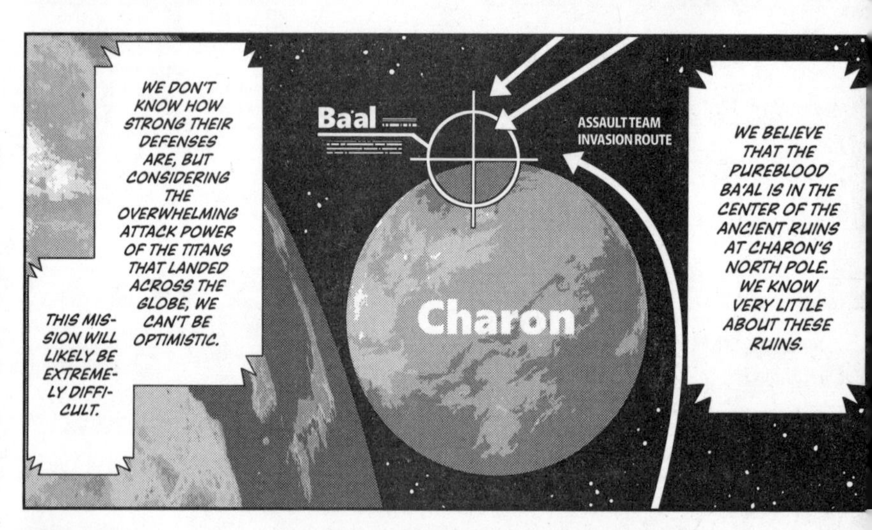
WE BELIEVE THAT THE PUREBLOOD BA'AL IS IN THE CENTER OF THE ANCIENT RUINS AT CHARON'S NORTH POLE. WE KNOW VERY LITTLE ABOUT THESE RUINS.
Ba'al
ASSAULT TEAM INVASION ROUTE
Charon
WE DON'T KNOW HOW STRONG THEIR DEFENSES ARE, BUT CONSIDERING THE OVERWHELMING ATTACK POWER OF THE TITANS THAT LANDED ACROSS THE GLOBE, WE CAN'T BE OPTIMISTIC.
THIS MISSION WILL LIKELY BE EXTREMELY DIFFICULT.

TEN MINUTES AGO, WE COMPLETED THE FORMATION OF AN ASSAULT TEAM MADE UP OF 760 OF OUR MOST CUTTING EDGE STARFIGHTERS.
YOUR JOB IS TO LEAD THE MISSION TO DEFEAT BA'AL...
...AND STOP HIS INVASION OF EARTH.

THIS BATTLE WILL DECIDE THE FATE OF MANKIND!
I WANT YOU TO PROCEED WHILE KEEPING THAT IN MIND!!
AYE, SIR!
YOU GOT IT.
YEAH!!
MM.
YES, SIR!
OKAY!
ALL ROUTES CLEAR!!
VRRRT
VRRRT
MISSION BEGINS IN 720!
YOU COULD JUST STAY OUT OF HUMAN AFFAIRS LIKE THE MONSTERS YOU ARE, BUT YOU HAVE TO REACH OUT!
YOU HAVE TO START TALKING ABOUT SAVING THE WORLD!

YOU DAMN IMMORTALS!
YOU MAKE ME WANT TO VOMIT!!
KEEP GOING, ALL OF YOU.
KEEP GOING... SANTA-KUN...
EXCUSE ME, KONOE-SAN!
HM?

I'M GARUDA PILOT COLONEL MAKINA AKASHI!
I WILL BE FLYING YOU TO THE ENEMY BASE! NICE TO MEET YOU!
UH, YEAH. THANKS!
I UNDERSTAND MY GREAT-GREAT-GRANDMOTHER OWES YOUR GRANDFATHER A LOT.
REALLY?

NOW, IF YOU'LL HURRY!
GOT IT!
TŌTA-KUN!

WE'RE ALL READY.
OKAY, LET'S GO!

HUH? YOU'RE PILOTING YOURSELF, JINBEI-SEMPAI?
I WAS AN ACE FLIER DURING THE FIRST AND SECOND WORLD WARS, AND THE MARS UPRISING.
A LITTLE MISSION LIKE THIS? PIECE OF CAKE.
KHEEEE
WAIT! DON'T LEAVE JUST YET!
JACOBS LADDER
JLP
WE FIGURED IT OUT!
WHAT YOUR GRANDFATHER LEFT YOU!
KIRIË! SANTA!
AND WE KNOW HOW TO USE IT, TOO!
NEGI-SAN'S SECRET WEAPON!
!
NEGI SPRINGFIELD'S OWN PERSONAL ARTIFACT, MILLE VINCULA.
SORRY WE HAD TO BUG YOU RIGHT AFTER YOU GOT BACK, BUT WITH YOUR MAGIC AUTHENTICATION AND THE MAGIC KEY WE FOUND, WE MANAGED TO OPEN IT UP, AND WE ALL ANALYZED IT TOGETHER.
WHAT WE FOUND INSIDE WAS A BUNCH OF ARTIFACTS.

IALDA HAS CAPTURED AND POSSESSED GENERATIONS OF VICTIMS THAT SHE HAS USED AS HER AVATARS.
WE FIGURED OUT THAT, BY COMBINING 17 OF THE ARTIFACTS IN THIS BOOK,
WE CAN BRING ONE OF THEM BACK.
I MEAN, YOUR GRANDPA WAS BASICALLY A GENIUS.

?!
BRING... BACK...
AND THAT MEANS!
YOU CAN GET YUKIHIME BACK, AND IALDA CAN'T DO ANYTHING TO STOP YOU.
JACOBS LADDER PROJECT

I CAN...
...GET YUKI-HIME BACK...?
CAN... CAN THAT REALLY BE...

HOO HEH HEH HEH. WELL? IT'S OKAY, YOU CAN SHOW YOUR HAPPINESS ON YOUR FACE.
UH, YEAH! I MEAN...
IT'S JUST SO HUGE, I HAVEN'T REALLY PRO-CESSED ...
TŌTA KONOE. THIS IS GOOD NEWS, BUT RIGHT NOW BA'AL COMES FIRST.
HE'S ALREADY ABSORBED 200 MILLION PEOPLE INTO HIS COSMO ENTELEKHEIA.
WE CANNOT ALLOW HIM TO CAUSE ANY MORE DAMAGE.

THINK ABOUT YUKIHIME LATER.
THE MISSION STARTS IN FIVE MINUTES.
Y...
YEAH, GOOD POINT!

ALL SHIPS, PREPARE FOR LAUNCH!!
ADVANCE DIVERSION SQUAD IS NOW IN POSITION ON THE CATAPULT!
VRRRT
VRRRT
VRRRT
MISSION BEGINS IN 240!!

TŌTA! WAIT! YOU FORGOT THIS! TAKE IT WITH YOU! HERE! THE NOTE-BOOK!
WHAT ?!
BUT IT'S NOT LIKE I CAN USE IT NOW...
JACOBS LADDER PROJECT
PLEASE! I HAVE A FEELING ABOUT THIS! A BAD FEELING, AND A GOOD ONE!
SWISH!
MRK.
PASH
OKAY. I BELIEVE IN YOU, KIRIË!
I'LL BE BACK!
MM.

TWO, ONE, ZERO.
COMMENCING OPERATION DAUNTLESS!!
ADVANCE DIVERSION SQUAD, LAUNCH!!
THWAP
THWAP
K-K-KZHNG
TŌTA-SAMA. SANTA-SAMA AND I WILL BE ACCOMPANYING YOU.
WE'LL CLEAR THE WAY FOR YOU!
THANKS! I'M HAPPY TO HAVE YOU! BUT DON'T PUSH YOURSELVES!

OKAY, COLONEL AKASHI! TAKE US OUT!!
YES, SIR!
AKASHI TEAM, READY!!

AKASHI TEAM, TAKING OFF!!
BOOM
07

THWAP
THWAP
THWAP
THE FATE OF MANKIND HANGS ON THIS BATTLE!!
WE PRAY FOR THE SUCCESS OF EACH AND EVERY ONE OF YOU!!
K-K-KSHING
キュキュキュ

I CAN SAVE HER...
I CAN SAVE YUKIHIME!!
AND IALDA CAN'T STOP ME!!

I'D NEVER EVEN CONSIDERED THE POSSIBILITY.
BOOM
GRANDPA, YOU REALLY ARE AWESOME!!

MISSION OBJECTIVE, CHARON'S NORTH POLE IN 180,000 KILOMETERS!
EEEEN
WE'RE PICKING UP INTENSIFIED HEAT READINGS IN THE VICINITY OF THE NORTH POLE! BE ON THE LOOKOUT FOR UNIDENTIFIED ATTACKS!
KHEE

MANA BOOST!
WHOOOOM
IGNITE AFTER-BURNERS!
IGNIT-ING!

WE'RE GOING TO BEAT BA'AL,
FIND IALDA, AND SAVE YUKIHIME!!
WOW. WE CAN DO THIS!! WE CAN TOTALLY DO THIS! WE CAN GET A HAPPY ENDING!!

JUST YOU WAIT, YUKI-HIME!!
BOOM
I'M ON MY WAY!!
I'LL BE THERE BEFORE YOU KNOW IT!!

悠
HOLDER!

UQ HOLDER!

STAFF

Ken Akamatsu

Takashi Takemoto

Kenichi Nakamura

Keiichi Yamashita

Yuri Sasaki

Madoka Akanuma

Thanks to Ran Ayanaga

UQ HOLDER!

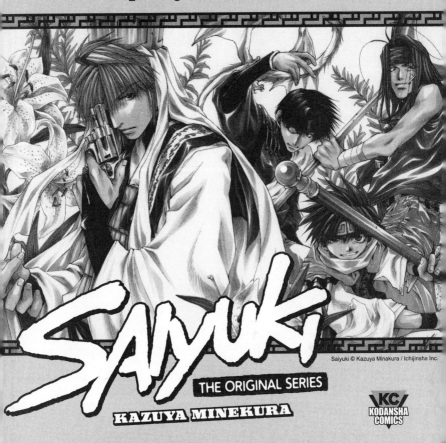

UQ HOLDER! 27 is a work of fiction. Names, characters, places, and incidents are the products of the author's imagination or are used fictitiously. Any resemblance to actual events, locales, or persons, living or dead, is entirely coincidental.

A Kodansha Comics Trade Paperback Original

Published in the United States by Kodansha Comics, an imprint of Kodansha USA Publishing, LLC, New York.

Publication rights for this English edition arranged through Kodansha Ltd., Tokyo.

First published in Japan in 2021 by Kodansha Ltd., Tokyo.

ISBN 978-1-64651-612-4

Printed in the United States of America.

www.kodansha.us
1st Printing

Translation: Alethea Nibley & Athena Nibley
Lettering: James Dashiell
Editing: David Yoo
Kodansha Comics edition cover design by Phil Balsman

Publisher: Kiichiro Sugawara

Director of publishing services: Ben Applegate
Director of publishing operations: Dave Barrett
Associate director of publishing operations: Stephen Pakula
Publishing services managing editors: Madison Salters, Alanna Ruse, with Grace Chen
Production manager: Emi Lotto